AN UNNAMED PRESS BOOK

Copyright © 2023 by Matthew Zapruder

www.unnamedpress.com

Unnamed Press, and the colophon, are registered trademarks of Unnamed Media LLC.

ISBN: 978-1-951213-68-8
eBook ISBN: 978-1-951213-80-0
LCCN: 2022949516

Cover design and typeset by Jaya Nicely

Manufactured in the United States of America by McNaughton & Gunn

Distributed by Publishers Group West

First Edition

2 4 6 8 10 9 7 5 3 1

Story of a Poem

a memoir

Matthew Zapruder

The Unnamed Press
Los Angeles, CA

This book is dedicated with love to my wife, Sarah, and our son, Simon. And with gratitude to poets Catherine Barnett, Matthew Rohrer, and Joshua Beckman, fellow travelers.

I think the sirens in *The Odyssey* sang *The Odyssey*, for there is nothing more seductive, more terrible, than the story of our own life, the one we do not want to hear and will do anything to listen to.

—*Mary Ruefle*

Poetry is everywhere; it just needs editing.

—*James Tate*

But the wind is our teacher.

—*Audre Lorde*

Story of a Poem

Prologue: Story

Once upon a time, two people met. It was summer, in a peaceful, mostly empty college town. It was evening, in a bar he had been to so many times, originally drawn by its mysterious, suggestive name. The Spoke. It sounded like a secret society, maybe of poets, which is what he had come to this small New England town to become. It took him many visits to notice the eponymous bikes from various eras hung on the walls, for he was not what you would call a "visual person."

The Spoke had cheap drinks, a large table in the back corner good for writing, and in the afternoon, light and dust interacted in a silent, one might even say poetic, way. Also, the parking lot backed directly onto the cemetery where Emily Dickinson was buried. He could take a break and walk back there and ask her for help, staring at her gray headstone, which she had in a poem presciently described as her "granite lip." Upon it was written the phrase *Called Back*.

He had been a student here in this small town, first for college then, after living elsewhere for several years, for graduate school in poetry. Now, after many years away again, he had returned as a teacher, in a week-long summer program. Everyone had gathered at that same bar where he had gone as a student. Without thinking, he placed himself back at his same table. He felt someone sit down next to him. He turned, and suddenly his presence in that bar felt fated. When she said her name, he felt he had known it all along. They began talking easily. She lived in San Francisco, he in New York. Their families had come from the same small region in the old country, and they nervously joked that they might be distant cousins. After the bar closed, they walked with a small group of people to Dickinson's grave, and, standing before it, earnestly recited some poems.

The next day they met up and wandered the deserted college town. A few days later he came to see her at her childhood home in Boston, where she was visiting her father, who engaged him in some requisite paternal harassment, quizzing him about deep Google results revealing certain inconsistencies in an intermittent employment history, then bringing him upstairs to demonstrate a working switchblade collection. She went back to San Francisco to her job as an urban planner, and he to New York, where he taught poetry at various institutions to graduate students.

A year later, he moved to San Francisco. They rented a small, dark apartment in North Beach. While she was at work, he went outside and walked past the brightly colored houses, many of them surrounded by scaffolding and wrapped in odd black gauze. The city seemed to be quietly waiting for a great calamity. He often walked down to the famous bookstore, all the way to the back and up the wooden staircase to the poetry room. The faces of the dead poets stared at him from the covers of books on tables and shelves.

It was so quiet, a few people sitting in corners and reading. He looked out the window over the avenue and watched the buses go by, the tourists weaving too slowly down the sidewalks while people dressed in professional clothing and sneakers impatiently tried to go around them. The majestic, forbidding, opaque blue-and-gold windows of the office buildings reminded him of his late father, who had worked as a lawyer in similar buildings in Washington, D.C. It was easy to imagine big decisions were being made behind them.

*

He had lived in San Francisco once before, in the early 1990s, after graduating from college then going to live for a year in the Soviet Union. As an undergraduate he had studied Russian, then received a fellowship, ostensibly to continue his senior thesis which gamely, albeit superficially, considered the work of a famous actor, songwriter and poet Vladimir Vysotsky, who could be described as a Slavic combination of Tom Waits, Bob Dylan, and James Dean. His fellowship would allow him to attend Moscow State University, a Stalinist monstrosity built in what was known as "wedding cake style." Thousands of students from all over the Soviet Union lived and studied in its interconnected wings. You could go from section to section, never exposing yourself to the elements, up and down the many floors. You could eat and shop without ever going outside, and find little clusters of every ethnic group within the USSR, each speaking their language, cooking their native food. It was easy to make friends quickly and get lost for hours, even days, in an Uzbek or Armenian microculture. There were just a handful of Americans there, all housed on the same floor, being watched, though it was easy to forget, since they were never bothered. It seemed no one really cared what anyone was doing anymore.

The USSR was in what no one at the time would have predicted was its final stage. Everything was literally and figuratively crumbling. Everyone was, even for Russians, deeply depressed. Most of the students at the university spent all day in their rooms, not going to class, drinking tea, then eventually vodka or what was called cognac but tasted more like that same vodka with cheap perfume dumped into it. There was almost nothing to eat, unless something from the black market would randomly appear, like a whole chicken that needed to be beheaded and plucked, or tangerines from Moldavia, probably radioactive.

Russian is a difficult language, because it conceives of central concepts—such as motion and time—in unique ways. Verbs are divided up into categories of repeated or singular actions, gradations of directionality, and distinctions in purpose that make little sense to a non-native speaker. Before he went to Russia, he would desperately memorize phrases with no idea why they were correct. When he first arrived, crucial linguistic concepts still eluded him, and he made laughable mistakes. Surrounded by native speakers, breathing in the language from everywhere, he began slowly to understand the language, not intellectually but intuitively. He found his awkward Russian gradually, then suddenly, becoming fluid and conversational. Not only could he speak, but his mind was changing: its categories, along with his sense of time and space themselves, were shifting.

Despite the progress he was making in the language, the omnipresent decay and futility permeated and threatened to overwhelm him. He began to feel he was becoming too lethargic to bother breaking down. He spent long hours playing a variation of backgammon, and wondering why he was there, other than to helplessly witness a society in despair. Suddenly, a month earlier than he was supposed to depart, he impulsively changed his plane ticket and left.

*

Exhausted, his body saturated with nicotine and ethanol and countless other impurities, he decided, without much thought, to move West. He tried Seattle, and eventually found his way south to California. Pre-internet San Francisco was an exotic destination, with no discernible industries, especially for a young person with no actual skills. It was where you went when you wanted to make nothing of yourself. He realized he wanted to check out completely from the competitiveness of the great American cities, where most of his other friends had gone. You could live in San Francisco for cheap, virtually unnoticed, and pursue your unformed, inconsequential dreams.

He got found a tiny room in a shared apartment. Some previous renter had painted the walls an unsettling, febrile orange. The leaseholder was the prickly and hilarious founder of an independent record label. Boxes of LPs by bands he remembered vaguely from his stint as a college radio DJ overflowed into the hallway. Other renters came and went: a recovering heroin addict who rode a bike one hundred miles a day to keep himself sober, a dark-haired young woman who would stand for hours, weeping, in the middle of the little concrete fenced-in area at the bottom of the wooden steps that led out the back door of the house. A mouse died unnoticed behind the stove and was found months later, cartoonishly flattened from desiccation.

The city was affordably between booms (his rent was $250 a month). He worked for a temp agency that provided substitute paralegal work. He and his friends, including his brother, were in various bands that seemed committed to creating complex and unlistenable songs that evaded basic musical structures and pleasures for no apparent reason. From those legal offices, very like the ones his father had worked in through his whole childhood, he stole supplies and made copies of flyers for shows no one attended. It seemed everyone was painting inscrutable canvases or making experimental films and projecting them on warehouse walls, while living in giant apartments, formerly grand homes now in states of gradual disrepair.

Every morning with his headphones on he walked to work through the Mission Dolores. Someone told him there used to be a creek that flowed where Mission Street was now, from the bay all the way to the Dolores church. He did not know then that he was walking over the place where the villages of the Ohlone had been. He and his friends walked or rode their bikes everywhere, obliviously, through neighborhoods where generations of native San Franciscans lived and worked. That summer, Nirvana poured from practically every window, and when the bartender put on the compact disc with the baby in the swimming pool chasing the dollar bill on the cover, everyone danced in manic, triumphant glee, convinced it was the start of a new era.

One time, his father had come for a single night, on a business trip. They had lunch at some expensive place and then walked around North Beach. His father loved City Lights Bookstore, so they went up wooden stairs to the poetry room and looked down onto Columbus Avenue. Then they went to a bar and had a late-afternoon drink, then a few more. They said virtually nothing of substance to each other. Then a long, silent, buzzed walk back to the father's hotel through the crowds of people heading home from work. It was getting dark, and the city was emptying.

*

After two years of working as a temp, paying cheap rent, being in a band that rehearsed all the time and almost never played shows, and aimlessly riding his bike around the city from coffee shop to bar to bar to bar, he felt anxious, starved for some kind of rigor and structure, or some engagement with art made not by his friends, or maybe just some conversations that did not dissolve inevitably into a spiritual fog. The only thing he could think of to do was to apply to graduate school.

He was accepted into a doctoral program in Slavic languages and literatures at UC Berkeley. His conversational Russian had disappeared, soon to be replaced by a stilted, artificial scholarly vocabulary. Long days sitting in the library, painstakingly translating texts about texts. Scraping at the very corner of an endless gray surface, revealing more gray, doomed to keep endlessly scraping. A giant clock, its immobile hands, the names of the great philosophers written in gold on the ceiling, motes of dust drifting around, the other bent-down heads.

He persevered for a year, then into a second. The exams to proceed to the PhD were notoriously, almost comically, difficult, with an impossibly extensive reading list. For hours candidates were grilled on the texts, sometimes in Russian, by the committee. Several professors had arcane scholarly specialties. One was an expert in Old Church Slavonic verb tenses, another in the literature of suicide. To prepare, he read every day, from 8 a.m. until midnight. At times, unable to absorb any more deep Slavic thoughts, he would stop and listen to Pavement's *Slanted and Enchanted*, staticky guitars and the possibility of being casually great. I was dressed for success, but success it never comes. He headed out to class and, passing a newspaper box, saw the headline that Kurt Cobain was dead. That was how he got the news. No internet at home, only at school, in the library, news on the street, the last days of writing letters.

*

One evening he wandered into a poetry reading on campus. He had, without thinking about it, almost automatically, been going to poetry events for a few years, sometimes at Berkeley but mostly at Cody's, the legendary bookstore on Telegraph Avenue. There were weekly readings upstairs, where famous poets would come to outdo each other. This was not the rhyming, romantic poetry he had read in high school, or the highly formal, extremely literary work he was reading in Russian. One week the legendary naturalist poet Gary Snyder read, and talked between poems with great earnestness about eating roadkill. Specific wildflowers and delicious crushed possum.

He would never have called himself a poet. At rare times he would start scribbling and would get interested in a clumsy, excited process, trying for as long as he could to keep away the feeling that this was ridiculous and he was wasting his time, which didn't feel precious at all. From the outside, at those moments, he would have seemed completely, uncharacteristically absorbed.

That night on campus, the Polish poet and Nobel laureate Czeslaw Milosz was reading. Milosz was an exile, observer of grand historical forces, preserver of those noble feelings that history is always busy failing fully to eradicate. After Milosz finished reading, everyone went into one of the classrooms, with a few tables with ancient cookies and new wine. He decided to go talk to the great poet, despite having recently and inexplicably dyed his hair a nauseating admixture of blue and green. This didn't seem visibly to bother Milosz, who graciously asked what he did. Without thinking about it, he said, for the first time, I am a poet. Milosz suddenly grabbed his hand, and, looking down, in a deep voice that thundered directly from his wild silver eyebrows, uttered, YOU MUST LEAVE.

He passed his exams, and did, then moved back to western Massachusetts, to go to poetry school. California an interlude, misremembered as a halcyon.

*

All those years later, as he walked again in San Francisco, in those same places, those times returned to him as if they were still somewhere happening. As he passed a certain doorway or street corner, memories would strike him with a startling reality and force. He felt, like a temporal breeze from unknown quarters, the memory of having nothing to do for days, no phone or internet or connection of any kind, of going places and just seeing who showed up.

They got married, under a tree on a hill. Mist came down from the headlands, freezing their friends and family, who had been warned by, and had ignored, the famous quote about the coldest winter being summer in San Francisco. Eventually they moved from North Beach across the bay, to Oakland, and a few years later had a child, a boy who eerily resembled his late grandfather, down to certain facial expressions and mannerisms.

It had been a long, difficult labor. Right after the birth, she had to be taken to surgery, and they handed the absurdly tiny bundle to the extremely new father and put the two of them into a chair, alone, in a room full of unidentifiable humming machines. All they said was, Put your pinkie finger in his mouth and turn your palm up and touch the top of his mouth, and he will happily latch on. And everything will be all right, we will come get you. The two of them sat there alone for hours. Perfectly calm, the boy stared up at his father with giant blue eyes taking in a bit of the world. For the first of countless times, the father thought, What are you thinking?

At last they wheeled her back into the room where the two of them were sitting. She would, as they had said, be all right; everything would be. The three of them went upstairs, for the first time a family. That night the boy slept all night on his father's chest. It was the only time in his life the father had felt his body was perfect, and not one time did he wish anything were different, or that he were elsewhere.

In photos from that first year you can see a giant smile, and in videos he is joyfully burbling along, focused and engaged. As he got a bit older, more and more often the father noticed that the boy would not participate in the activities into which the other kids his age seemed so easily to slip. Instead of dutifully sitting in a circle at the little kid gymnasium, singing the horrible songs and discussing pretend pizza, he would roam the rest of the room, jumping and exploring and singing his own favorite tunes. The father completely related to his disinterest, while experiencing a growing dread. The father kept his thoughts to himself, especially since he was by nature a melancholy catastrophizer.

The father was giving the boy a bath, watching him recite a favorite book, from start to finish, word for word. The boy looked up into the air, somewhere past his father's shoulder, his eyes elsewhere. It was clear he was actually seeing an image of the book, as if it were hovering before him. He looked like he was mentally flipping the pages, remembering the pictures and what words went with each one. There was a place he could go in his mind that was so real it was impossible to resist, an immersion so total and deep. It was impossible for the father or anyone else to reach him there, in his absorption and pleasure.

*

Father and son would lie next to each other at bedtime. Night after night, the father gently squeezing his son's hand, wanting nothing other than for him to squeeze it back. They had put up some glow-in-the-dark stars on the wall, and the son looked up and laughed, and said, "Star!" The father kept trying to get him to say it again, the son listened and listened, but he wouldn't, not for a long time.

Every morning the father would wake up early with him and sit in the living room. They would look out the window at the cars passing by on the busy street. The father would strap him into the stroller and push him a few blocks to a coffee shop, where he was known as "the chill baby." They would sit outside while the father drank his coffee and made conversation with various people. No one liked Hillary. The boy chattered to himself, happily repeating the words of his favorite books, smiling at the world.

The election at last arrived, bringing its shocking, retroactively predictable result. People gathered at Lake Merritt, a lagoon in the middle of Oakland that serves as the unofficial central public space of the city. The father lifted his son high in the air so he could see the signs, the lake, the thousands holding hands, and hear everyone singing "Imagine." A few weeks later, in early December, a terrible fire consumed a warehouse known as the Ghost Ship, killing thirty-six people, many of them young artists who were trying to find a new way to live together, collectively, to support each other in the making of art in an unaffordable city. People gathered a second time at the lake. Again they sang and held up signs, with which everyone helplessly agreed.

That night after the second gathering, he sat heavily on his couch. The two of them were at last asleep above him. He drank, numbing himself, listening to the sounds of the helicopters as they continued to surveil the area for potential demonstrations or highway shutdowns.

DECEMBER

At first we all
went down to the lake
to hold hands,
all the multicolored
signs said
with love
we will resist,
over my head
I lifted my son

so he could see
what people
look like
when they hear
the song *Imagine*,
a few weeks later
again people stood
at the water,
this time at night
holding flashlights
to say to fire
you came
without permission
and took our young
gentle soldiers
for art
so we will show
even with our old
technology
we can see
each other
without you,
others booed
the mayor which was
my friend said
understandable,
I don't know
what is anymore,
everyone understands
in a different
contradictory way
the so far purely
abstract
catastrophe
so many millions
of choices
brought us,

not too far
from the water
I sat on the couch
below the sound
of blades
drinking amber
numbing fluid
my thoughts
chopping the air
feeling not
what is the word
to be a father
equipped,
mine never told me
where to hide
a brick of gold,
for a long time
I have known
no voices
will come at last
to tell us how
to stop pretending
we don't know
if it is not
safe for some
it is not
for anyone.

(from *Father's Day*)

A few weeks later, the three of them went into a pretty little
house in Berkeley that had been converted to offices. A grimly cheer-
ful woman greeted them with a familiar, efficient accent, maybe
Swiss. She took out a bunch of toys and spread them on a table, and
asked the two-year-old some questions, which he did not answer,

choosing instead to walk over to the door, turning the knob again and again. She played with him for an hour, running through some tests, asking him to give her things, to tell her his name, to point. He did not seem to hear.

That office, the father noticed, was only one block away from that first place he ever lived by himself, back during that time he was studying Russian in graduate school, a little apartment with an arch of flowers. They left, the boy happily babbling away, repeating words from his favorite books.

A few days later, walking back to that office with her for a second time, just the two of them, he had the vertiginous feeling that if he could stand above his life, tracing his movements from the apartment he had rented in 1993, back east and everywhere else, then returning here, he would see a giant, queasy oval, closing at last. When they heard the diagnosis, they held each other and uncontrollably wept. Then went home and began making phone calls, arranging various interventions and supports, trying to understand what to do about school, about speech therapy, beginning a long process of understanding that does not end.

Everything was different from what the other families they knew were going through, much more complicated, full of decisions to make and logistics to arrange. The gulf between their little family and their friends who had kids the same age became apparent, and continued to grow. The stress and pressure and uncertainty often felt literally unbearable. They took turns falling apart. They often felt like partners in a gradually failing business that had no discernible project other than continuing to exist, or perhaps to receive well-meaning, ineffectual sympathy.

They had been stars in school, high achievers who went to colleges with impressive names, and had succeeded professionally at the highest levels. Now they were on the other side of that wall. The grievous limitations of the pervasive, ruthless meritocratic machine into which they had so willingly and unquestioningly inserted themselves, in order to emerge on the other end as highly valued products, became painfully obvious. The experience of being people who needed help and often merited compassion felt intolerable and utterly necessary.

The love he felt for his son collided practically every moment with intense fear and exhaustion. So many things that came easily to other children—speech, social play, a naturally growing understanding of the world—had to be painstakingly broken down into steps and taught. Sometimes there was no discernible progress. What seemed to be joyful for other parents was such a source of worry. All this permeated not just by intense love, but also admiration for his son's joyful spirit, his fierce affection for those close to him, his sensitivity to music, his astounding memory, his joy and facility in building . . . what did it all mean? Where was it going? Those questions could not be silenced, and there could be no answers.

There is a singular terror when the story is suddenly taken away, and one is left in a new life. The future at last reveals itself as it has always been: vast and uncertain and full of a range of irreconcilable possibilities. He thought he had been ready to accept whatever future would come. Now, however unprepared he was, he knew that the fragility of that story was itself the true story, one that everyone, including the new parents who surrounded him, whether they knew it or not, were now in too.

*

For months he had been drinking gradually larger bottles of various forms of alcohol mixed into noxious concoctions, by himself, in the evenings, watching television shows that the next day he could not remember. His mood had now worsened into something close to a depression. He was turning in very small circles within an ominous whirlpool. Even as he went capably through the motions, completing all his tasks for work, for his son, he felt less and less capable of surviving his own life.

In despair, in confusion, often hungover, he kept writing, a few poems here and there. Then, during the summer of 2018, he began to force himself to write each day. He and his friend Matt, who lived in Brooklyn, agreed to send each other new poems every morning. At first it was painful. Then, suddenly, impossibly, to sit down and write became his greatest relief. The poems began to come with ease, as if they had been waiting to be written. When the summer ended, he had many new poems, almost a book. But something still was missing.

At the start of November, after a series of evenings he could only hazily remember, he decided it was at last time to stop drinking. This decision came to him with a sudden, rare clarity. He felt both terrified and calm. To finish the book of poetry, he decided to write a single poem, as slowly as possible, and to preserve its drafts. He would write in prose about this process of making a poem, while it was happening. Poems, writes Audre Lorde, "are carved from the rock experiences of our daily lives." What would it be like to tell the story of this carving, of making a single poem, and to write about all the stuff in life that surrounded and informed its gradual, halting construction?

This was very possibly an epically terrible idea, one that in its self-consciousness would make it impossible for him to finish the poem at all. But his instinct told him he needed a new form, not just the poem or prose, but both together.

What is the relation between making poems and learning to be the father of this atypical child? It felt to him like the same struggle, something he had been trying to learn for so long in his writing and now had to learn in his life. An irresistible force, which could be called love, always drew him back to poetry, to searching out what was strange and beautiful and mysterious and new in language, and trying to make a place for it. That same force, something he felt every time he looked at his son, made him want to change himself, and the world.

That fall, everyone was talking about the migrant children, separated from their parents, in concentration camps on our southern border. He kept thinking, What is happening to the autistic children? Why does no one ever mention them? Do the other kids take care of them? Where are they right now? The news, what Wallace Stevens called "the pressure of the real," so often felt psychologically and spiritually intolerable. Yet everyone kept on living.

That fall was a season of terrible fires. He wrote every day for many months. He worked on the poem, then put it away, then came back to it again. He wrote about his life at the time, his fears, his memories. Other new poems came, and poems were revised. He watched society tearing itself apart at the very moment it most needed solidarity. Everyone on social media, his students, even his closest friends seemed ready to explode into anger at each other. He often felt foolish working on the poem, and writing about writing it, but could not ever fully leave it alone.

11.5.18

```
when it's still dark
  I rise and know
all night
    I didnot rest
next to her worries
  I am sitting
  at the prow
 watching  the sky
 behind me
in the redwoods
two sleeps
watch over
our house
vast and lonely
with unconcern
  they have seen
 many kingdoms
 green in glory
 arise and go
      I rise and know
    it is our turn
```

tv. sleepi

I Woke Up in California (First Draft)

It's 5 a.m., and the busy street is quiet. Outside the window, the leaves of the trees are black. Wires slice through the darkness, making dark shapes. The sky gradually becomes visible. I can feel Sarah and Simon still asleep in the rooms behind me. For a moment I can almost imagine I'm at the prow of a ship, sitting still as the world rotates into unhelpful light. A little tremor shakes the desk and I feel a flash of panic, but it's not an earthquake, just a lone truck passing.

Last night as I was putting him to bed I told him that something would happen in "two sleeps." It's something I've heard other parents say, and I found it coming out of my mouth. I didn't know if he'd heard me, lost as he so often was in singing one of his favorite songs. Often he will seem not to hear, but then a few hours or days later will repeat what was said, or answer a question asked minutes or even hours ago. Sometimes months later, he will repeat something I said to him, laughing. It's as if he and I are in an endless conversation, the pace of which is slower than I could ever have imagined.

All summer, I had been writing a new poem every morning and emailing it to Matt. He would send me a new poem back too. I told myself, and believed, these were just practice for what would eventually be the "real" writing. A neat trick, impossible to deliberately replicate. I never had a plan, or any idea where to begin. I would sometimes choose a phrase that seemed to glow with at least a little potential.

This autumn morning, I remember Matt once showed me how you can start a poem by putting one or two lines in the middle of the page, and then writing out from them, alternating a line before, and then one after. He said this method came to him in a dream. It's always better to start with a phrase, however ordinary, than an idea, however grand.

"Two sleeps," I type, in the middle of the page. Then roll the platen up one line to type above it, something that could make sense as a line before. Then back down, to type something that could go after: "in the redwoods/ two sleeps/ watch over ..." Watch over what, I don't know.

It's just a beginning, but as Bob Hass says, you can't revise nothing. Not until nothing becomes a few words. When you have no ideas, or too many, it's best to find a few words that seem to have potential, for now inexplicable. The painter Degas once said to his friend Mallarmé, I want to write poems, but I have too many ideas. Mallarmé replied: Poems, my dear Degas, are not made of ideas, but of words. "Poetry makes nothing happen," W. H. Auden wrote, which doesn't mean it *does* nothing. It makes nothing *happen*. It activates the silence. You begin, and now there is something to listen to.

*

There's a huge new wildfire north of us. It is, we are told, "far away," near a place called Paradise, once again suggesting we live in a cruel simulation. I go outside to check the air. It's already brown, a color tinted with the remnants of a burned tree, giving everything a sepia apocalyptic feel. The sun a little magenta disc I stare directly at with useless impunity. Winter in the Arctic; permanent twilight. Not good for any lungs, though it does paradoxically make me want to have an anachronistic smoke. Through my mask I can hear my breathing.

Keats called autumn the season of mellow mists and fruitfulness. In California the season of mists is summer, and autumn the season of fires. Starting earlier and earlier every year, the faint scent of smoke, white ash on the windshield. Always as if a candle has just been blown out. The sun dimmed, the darkening air. The constant calibration: How far away? How fast? The masks. Like so many things, it wasn't this way before, but will be now.

Not for the first time I think, scouring social media to find out more about the fire, can these geniuses of the algorithm, the ones who figured out how to permit us to willingly turn our attention and friendship into money, how to let us monetize for them every moment of our lives not already devoted to tasks, at least use their math to figure out where the next fire will begin? Where the lightning is most likely to strike, where the ground is most hospitable to disaster? That way at least we could be waiting there with some water. Now that we've given them everything for free, is that too much to ask?

*

I put on my N95 and wipe ash off the windshield, as I've done so many times since summer, when those white flakes began to appear, drifting from the north. At first I barely noticed. I drive to visit a friend's class, the air now fully umber. Inside, the air filtered, a low, fragile hum. This morning I learned Paradise was completely burned. It feels soulless to point out how overdetermined this sounds. Nine people died, making it the deadliest wildfire in California history.

Isn't it a privilege, a student asks, to write poems when the world is burning? I answer, too quickly, *Yes.* I didn't mean to sound exactly as I must have, dismissive and snide. I add, in an attempt to convey the sincerity I actually feel, Can we imagine we need to protect, rather than condemn, that privilege in each other?

They look at me. I should have said, I want to give you some way of protecting yourselves, but I don't know how.

I should have said, I think of the poem as a physical space, a giant museum or a forest. I go in and listen. I hear something, write it down, and emerge, hopefully for the better changed.

I should have said, I have to do this to survive. Otherwise my life is an endless version of my childhood, everyone dinner-table arguing as if their lives depended on it, which in some way they did. As if it mattered what we decided about some giant philosophical issue. We waited impatiently around the wooden table, not listening, for someone to stop speaking, so it could be our turn. And despite everything, I also feel affection, even longing, for all that argument and complicated love, that lit-up dining room in the suburbs, surrounded by trees in the dark.

*

This morning, I want to stop working on the poem and write something else. I think of my friend, thousands of miles away. The ninth-century Tang dynasty poets (Li Bai, Du Fu, Wei Ying-wu) used to write each other poems of friendship, sometimes leaving them on the walls of structures where they knew their friends might later return, to console themselves in their endless wandering.

I wrote a new poem quickly. The first draft included the lines "We were sadder / than Chinese poets / of the 9th century." I love the T'ang dynasty poets of that era: Li Bai, Du Fu, Li Shang-yin, Wei Ying-wu, though of course since I don't know Chinese I can only read them in translation. They lived in a time of a great empire, beset by political turmoil, and eventually a civil war. It often seems to me we are headed, inevitably, for such instability and disruption.

When I was very young, first starting to write, I used to think that facts, or the truth, didn't matter at all in poems. I just wanted to write something strange, exciting, mysterious, resonant, new. Facts were for encyclopedias. Only later did I come to realize how often facts are more fantastical than anything we could invent. And also, as my own relationships deepened, the truth, of my own life and of the lives of others, became more important to me. What I wrote was no longer separate from me. Now what I say in poems is inextricable from who I am. Maybe this means I am less free to invent, but I don't think so. I think it means I am freer to listen, and to discover.

Nevertheless, a fact or a truth in a poem can land with a kind of thud. In such cases, I trust my ear. I listen and try to find exactly where the dead spot is. This is not a matter of intellect or memory. Beneath the initial fact, or adjacent to it, there is something even more resonant, even truer. Did it really matter that I had thought, initially, of the 9th century Chinese poets when writing the first draft? That was the first thought, based on remembered facts. But something about that line did not feel right in my ear and mouth, even though (or maybe because) it was merely correct. Then I remembered the dynasty subsequent to the Tang was known as the Northern Song.

THE PLEDGE

Yesterday I kicked a tree
a walnut fell in a grave
nobody got hurt

it's June
the February
of summer

alone in Oakland
cleaning white ash
from not-so-distant fires

off my windshield
with my sleeve
I think of you

far, old friend,
scribbling poems
in the park

to your wife
and saying them
happily to no one

do you remember
when we pledged
to always look?

we were sadder
than Chinese poets
of the Northern Song

like them
in desperate times
we drank a lake

sized amount of wine,
which made us strong
because we knew

no matter how much
everything matters
our poems can always

be read by anyone

(from *Father's Day*)

In October 1928, in Granada, Federico García Lorca strode up
to a stage in the middle of wild applause. I have imagined it many
times. The hall of the Granada Athenaeum decorated with flowers
and tapestries. Many in the audience holding bouquets, their ex-
pectant faces turned up toward the stage. The candlelit magic of a
ritual. They had come to hear Lorca, author of the book of poems
and drawings *Romancero Gitano*, give a lecture on the poetic imag-
ination. The black piano gleaming, so Lorca could stop at times
to play and sing Andalusian folk songs he had learned as a child,
growing up in a small town in the middle of the vega.

"Imagination, Inspiration, Evasion" is not even really a lecture.
It is a reflection of Lorca's mind, an enactment of what it is like
to think as a poet. He explores the idea that writing poetry is not
about inventing, but discovering:

> The human imagination invented giants in order to attri-
> bute to them the construction of great grottoes or enchanted
> cities. Later, reality taught us that those great caves are
> made by the drop of water. The pure, patient, eternal drop
> of water. In this case, as in many others, reality wins. After
> all, it is much more beautiful that a cave be a mysterious
> caprice of water—chained and ordered by eternal laws—
> than the whim of giants who have no other meaning than
> that of an explanation.

A mysterious caprice of water. This is the human mind encountering reality, and according to Lorca, it is far more beautiful than some arbitrary explanation, mere imagining.

Of the early twentieth-century French surrealists, Wallace Stevens wrote, "To make a clam play an accordion is to invent not discover." I love the surrealists, the hope they had that we could heal ourselves through dreaming. When we were children, we made no distinction between that dream world and our "real" experiences. We were filled with wonder. Of course we were also cruel. We lacked adult perspective. The purpose of poetry was to heal this great wound in our consciousness. We would become like children again, except also wise. By reconnecting the part of ourselves that dreams with the rest of us, we would remember that we are all human, that the entire world is alive. We would never start another war again. Of course, this did not work. But in that hope they wrote some of my favorite poems. The earth is blue like an orange. I have so often dreamed of you, my wife with thoughts of summer lightning.

Yet I think Stevens has a point, at least about an aspect of their poetry, and while I adore their freedom, I dread replicating such irrelevancy, as I equally dread an earnest moral hectoring. I do wish I could see that clam, though.

*

I have always loved words for what they can do, and for all the different things they can mean. I love how they feel in my mouth. In that way, I am like all writers I know. I am also very like my son. Now that I have become the parent of a son who is working so hard to achieve fluency in language, my respect for communication in all aspects of my life has increased. The simple act of reaching out in writing to say something to you, and you hearing me, and then responding, even if only in my imagination because you are far away and I will most likely never know you, feels even more holy to me.

Poetry gives us the great gift of allowing us to forget, momentarily, that communicating is mostly functional. If we allow language to drift away from us, and don't try to use but rather follow it, we can discover something. It is as if the imagination is more like a tool, or a sense like sight or hearing or memory, a deeper faculty, something that opens up the world to the poet and reader. When properly understood and deployed, the imagination can uncover truths that are not available elsewhere.

According to Lorca, a lesser poet settles for merely imagining. A great poet is inspired, that is, breathed into by some force outside themselves.

For me, imagination is synonymous with discovery.

I do not believe in creation but in discovery, and I don't believe in the seated artist but in the one who is walking down the road.

The poetic imagination travels and transforms things, giving them their purest meaning, and it defines relationships no one had suspected.

Poetry is like faith—it isn't meant to be understood but to be received in a state of grace.

In the lecture, Lorca also says:

The mechanics of the poetic imagination are always the same: a concentration, a leap, a flight, a return with the treasure, and a classification and selection of what has been brought back.

First, the pure, empty desire to make something. A concentration, which is really a separation from the world, a decision to think about . . . nothing. Nothing to say, nothing to do, other than leap. A leap is a pushing away of the earth. No more, no, that is not how the world is, it cannot be like this any longer. An initial rejection, explicit or implicit, of some widely agreed-upon truth, or just the usual way of doing things. The beginning is a call to go a different way. The poem creates a new space of freedom in which to question and dream. In this way, poetry is by its nature oriented toward strangeness, revolution. What appears dire can be thrilling and beautiful and subject to change.

Some time passes. If I am lucky enough to forget everything else, this is the time of greatest pleasure. That place you go after the leap, and what happens there, Lorca does not name. It is particular to each of us. Someone (a student, a fellow poet, oneself) can only be directed there, or maybe with the utmost dispassionate gentleness pushed off the ledge, for them to discover that it is possible to soar for a while. But once one has leapt, and is flying, and hunting, what is instinctively, intuitively, feelingly chosen, and how, and where: that is the part of the process that cannot be taught, only provoked.

I want to sleep the sleep of the apples, Lorca writes. My heart of silk is filled with lights, with lost bells, with lilies and bees. I will go very far, farther than those hills.

More and more often I think the rare treasure I gather in writing poems is the awareness I would not have without writing them. Can that state of awareness be communicated through a poem? Can the poem be a secret machine, carried on a little scrap of paper or hidden in the mind, so one can always have a place to rest, to resist?

I also hope for the possibility of communion, both with the hidden parts of myself and with imagined readers. One can believe for a moment that one is no longer lonely. The poet, says Lorca, wants. "We all want. But this is his sin: to want. One shouldn't want, one should love." I want to be someone Lorca believes in, the poet walking the road, listening, but I am trapped inside by the terrible air.

*

Richard Hugo writes, "When you start to write, you carry to the page one of two attitudes, though you may not be aware of it. One is that all music must conform to truth. The other, that all truth must conform to music. If you believe the first, you are making your job very difficult ..."

When I first started to write poems, I carried both attitudes with me. I believed, on the one hand, that music must conform to truth: you start with what you want to say, and use "music" to convey it in the most powerful way. This sounds, when I think of it, dangerously like advertising, or propaganda. At the same time, I was looking to write not in order to convey a message, but to search for, and submit to, a different kind of music: a deeper order or significance, an intimated truth that could not otherwise be felt. And I believed this deeper order could only be found through intuition. I had to completely trust and defer to it. This presumably would lead to deeper, "poetic" knowledge.

This unresolved contradiction within me made things, as Hugo points out, very difficult. For hours I would sit, scratching my head, writing down a few words and then erasing them. Was I supposed to be saying something I already knew in the most beautiful possible way? Or trying to follow music, to find out what I did not know I believed? And if the latter, how was I supposed to write without controlling what I wrote? Wouldn't that lead to complete gibberish?

I was working at cross-purposes. The poems I wrote to express what I already knew felt dead on the page. I was coming up with decorated language to say what could be more directly said. But I didn't know what else to do, how to create the mystery and strangeness in the poems that I loved. The poems I read by others and loved the most seemed so clear, but full of something that was somehow outside the writer, as if the poet were channeling something.

I have come to believe that writing is an endless, shifting negotiation between intention and discovery, ideas brought to the page and ones uncovered in the process of writing itself, music and truth. Sometimes I know what I want to say. Almost always, I can only really discover what I think and believe through the process of writing the poem. I have to let myself be ok with both states, and to shift freely between them. I have to let myself make mistakes, be foolish and wrong, to write things down that make no sense but seem beautiful or funny or weird, and then use my intuition to guide me to what feels truthful to me.

My father was an extremely analytical man, a lawyer who thrived on success, achievement, and the clear articulation of goals. Beneath that controlled, friendly, warm exterior self he showed to the world, was an immense amount of hidden emotion, which only rarely surfaced. He loved sailing, an unlikely hobby (or perhaps not) for a Jewish son of immigrant dressmakers, especially one who had grown up landlocked in Dallas, and then gone even farther inland to University of Oklahoma for college. When I was a kid, in the summer he liked to rent little boats called Sunfishes and sail them in smallish New England ponds or harbors. I didn't like it as much, but would sometimes go with him. He used to hand me the wooden tiller and tell me to pick some destination on the horizon, a house or notable tree, and try to just keep guiding the boat vaguely there. It wasn't necessary to stay exactly on target, and in fact, keeping the boat too rigidly pointed could lead to a lot of unnecessary jerking around of the tiller. More than the sun and the wind and the water, the sound of the wavelets slapping against the hull, the peace and distance from land and its obligations, I think he got such pleasure out of having to steer this way, then teaching me how to do it. There was a lot of feel involved, and forgiveness. Go easy, he would say, and no sudden movements. Almost always the choice of goal was arbitrary, and anyway the point was to be together as long as possible.

*

I wrote these lines twenty-three years ago, at the beginning of poetry graduate school, in a rickety house on School Street:

Some blue panes
hang in the sky
long after the buildings that held them.

One of those names
I kept many nights in my pocket
till I whispered it over a stream
too small for its own.

I sit by the wall.
I have sewn a bag from wet leaves.
I reach in blind with my mouth's thick fingers.

Whatever I say there grows a white flower.
Under the path of two swallows,
the path of two swallows grows a white flower.

Such things vow to never be named,

bowing their heads

as if that would save them.

Beyond my father, and his father, who died when I was two (all my memories are from photographs), there is a silence. The same with my mother's family, though I knew my maternal grandfather, who lived until I was in my twenties. A few names of people and towns, some scraps of family history told around the dinner table, random anecdotes. Untethered flashes of images translated into the visual from stories we have been told. A mother and her children, without the father, standing and waiting for a train to take them somewhere so they could get on a boat. Peasant Jews, practically starving in the winter, living near a little town called Covel in what is now the Ukraine but then was called White Russia. Rich Jews in a warm house in a city (Budapest?), with white tablecloths and many books, suddenly deciding to go, taking almost nothing, ending up in Pittsburgh.

It's quite probable that my lack of connection was not merely personal, but also historical. Nothing connected me to a past beyond my childhood. A great trauma had been erased, and was hardly spoken of. I had no tree. Where had I fallen from?

The rest of the poem, which I will not reproduce, is melodramatic. It's "about" the imagined history of my family in Europe and Russia, before they were murdered or went into exile. It was too huge a subject, at least for this young poet, and immediately drew me into falseness, self-dramatization, and maudlin magical realism. The problem is not in the lines, but in the frame, which ignores the central impossibility of knowing anything at all about my particular past, of a world completely destroyed, without record or remnants. The problem, which is that I cannot truly know what I am writing about, is evaded, instead of placed in the poem.

These lines are more than a little sentimental: someone once told me never to use *whisper* in a poem, which is always good advice, until it is not. But there is also a weird prescient clarity to the idea that the windows of a destroyed building would remain even after the building is gone. And to the idea that these windows might be equivalent to lost names. A somewhat attenuated chaining of ideas, yes, but there's an elusive truth to it. And a desire to hear these names spoken, which can never be assuaged.

Our last name, some say, refers to the Prut, a river that makes a giant looping U shape from Hungary through Moldova and up to the Danube. *Za Prut* could mean *beyond the Prut River*, or beyond the pond (*Prud* in Russian), There is also a Russian word *zaprud*, meaning a dam. So something to do with water for sure. People have trouble saying it. We say, It is pronounced just like it is spelled, while secretly knowing how ridiculous that sounds.

I think in this recovered poem I was writing about writing about the past, a past I had constructed out of partial knowledge (the bag of wet leaves, into which I am reaching with "my mouth's thick fingers"). Looking at it so many years later, it feels genuine to me. But it also doesn't really gather enough force to be more than an early draft.

In these few lines I can see a lucidity of song that, were I to write them now, I would trust as the real moments in the poem, the purpose toward which I was writing, without knowing it.

*

I still have a book I read with religious frequency at that time, its orange cover now faded by decades of sunlight. *Poems of Paul Celan* was full of poems I did not understand. Yet when I read them, I felt a deep connection, and I knew they were doing something I wanted to do in my own poems, but couldn't yet.

Celan (an anagram of his surname, Ancel) was, like my maternal grandmother's family, a Jew from Romania. In America, Jews from there were looked down on by those who once lived closer to the great cities, especially Budapest and Berlin, and who revered the Austro-Hungarian culture, and the German language above all. Celan's parents were murdered in the Holocaust, and he was tormented his whole life by the fact that he felt condemned to write in German. That was his birth language, and it contained all of his memory, wordless and otherwise.

Celan has a reputation for writing "difficult" poetry. I did not know that when I first read his poems. I just accepted them. "Assisi" is about the town in Umbria where Saint Francis had his hermitage, and where the great frescoes of Giotto are:

Umbrian night.
Umbrian night with the silver of churchbell and olive leaf.
Umbrian night with the stone you carried here.
Umbrian night with the stone.

Who is the "you" carrying the stone? We don't know until the end of the poem, when it becomes clear that it is Saint Francis who is being addressed:

Brightness that will not comfort, brightness you shed.
Still they are begging, Francis — the dead.

I adore any poem that mentions a name. Like when Frank O'Hara reports that in "A True Account of Talking to the Sun at Fire Island," the sun came to him and said, using a bad pun:

"Frankly I wanted to tell you
I like your poetry. I see a lot

on my rounds and you're okay. You may
not be the greatest thing on earth, but
you're different . . ."

Or Coleridge at the end of "This Lime-Tree Bower My Prison,"
who imagines his friend looking up at the day's last rook (basically
a crow, but with distinguishing whitish feathers on its face) and
writes that he hopes that it flew over his head and

> . . . had a charm
> For thee, my gentle-hearted Charles, to whom
> No sound is dissonant which tells of Life.

Celan's poem for the surrealist Paul Éluard, one of his greatest,
doesn't mention Éluard's name:

In Memoriam Paul Éluard

Lay those words into the dead man's grave
which he spoke in order to live.
Pillow his head amid them,
let him feel
the tongues of longing,
the tongs.

Lay that word on the dead man's eyelids
which he refused to him
who addressed him as thou,
the word
his leaping heart-blood passed by
when a hand as bare as his own
knotted him who addressed him as thou

into the trees of the future.

Lay this word on his eyelids:
perhaps
his eye, still blue, will assume
a second, more alien blueness,
and he who addressed him as thou
will dream with him. We.

The syntax is exhilarating and devastating. Syntax is my most secret and essential love in poetry. Its magic enacts or reveals truths unavailable elsewhere.

In the second stanza it takes a few readings for me to understand "which he refused to him." I need to slow down to see that "which" refers to the nearest antecedent, "eyelids." Éluard refused to show his eyelids—that is, close his eyes—to anyone who called him "thou." It's a double negative. The refusal is something positive: he kept his eyes open to anyone who was intimate with him, who called him "thou." It is a tribute to the way Éluard returned intimacy. The trees of the future!

And that solitary "We" at the end . . . an assertion of the possibility of the collective, which means so much more when we remember all that Celan lost to the Nazis, who exploited that concept of *we versus they* to the most homicidal and nihilistic of purposes. A pronoun can be launched out to unknown readers, not in easy assumption but in desperate hope of solidarity and connection.

"Matiere de Bretagne" ("Matter of Britain") has one of the most remarkable endings of a poem I have ever read:

You
you teach
you teach your hands

you teach your hands you teach
you teach your hands
　　how to sleep

Who did he mean by this "you"? Reading it, I know he meant me. I feel the truth of this poem physically. I think you could only end one poem this way in your whole life; it is almost too much, too dramatic, but if you come upon it suddenly (as a poet or a reader) without preparation, it feels completely authentic.

When I first read the poem, I didn't understand the title "Matter of Britain." I don't remember if I looked it up, but now I easily can on my device. According to Wikipedia (let no one say that poets do no research), "The Matter of Britain" is "one of the three great story cycles recalled repeatedly in medieval literature, together with the Matter of France, which concerned the legends of Charlemagne, and the Matter of Rome, which included material derived from or inspired by classical mythology." The Matter of Britain contains the Arthurian cycle: Camelot and the quests for the Holy Grail. The rest of the poem leading up to the end makes far more sense to me now.

Celan is best known for "Death Fugue," the most famous poem about the Holocaust. "Black milk of daybreak we drink it at sundown," the poem begins, and it is clear it is spoken in voices of murdered Jews, and also of those who live in the aftermath. There is a man who plays with serpents, a golden-haired Margarete who symbolically stands in for Germany, and opposed to them Shulamit with ashen hair. Mysterious phrases I could not stop thinking about repeat in the fugue. We dig a grave in the breezes. Death is a master from Germany.

Celan later repudiated this poem as an artistic portrait of a suffering that should never be captured in something manageably beautiful. His later poetry became thorny, disjointed, highly symbolic without any overt referent, and, if it strikes a reader at the right time, especially late at night when all categories start to dissolve and the darkness outside the window takes on a sentient, palpable force, immensely powerful.

His short, untitled poems haunted me. I still can't explain why. He asks to be taken up into little night, "three pain-inches above the / floor." He says to the reader, to me, "listen your way in / with your mouth."

*

When I was in my twenties, my grandparents finally moved out of the house my mother had grown up in. In the attic where we used to sleep as kids, and where my grandfather would come in at bedtime and sing "Goodnight, Irene" to me and my younger brother and sister, in a row in our little cots, I had found her typewriter, a Royal Quiet Deluxe, perfectly preserved from her high school days. My grandfather was the sort of person who would make sure it was in pristine working order, and when I opened the case, the keys gleamed. It didn't even need a new ribbon. It made a satisfying, well-oiled clack.

I lugged it to the house I was living in on School Street, in Northampton, Massachusetts. I had moved back from California to the same weird little valley where I had gone to college, to go to poetry graduate school. Thankfully I did not yet know that a manual typewriter was a writerly cliché. For a while, the typewriter just sat there in the corner of my room.

I was still toiling away, writing a lot of poems the way I used to: choose a subject, and try to write something "about" it. Use a computer. Those poems always felt labored and ponderous. No matter what I said, the thoughts in them were never new. Nothing was being added by my writing. I had already figured it out, and mostly it was banal and obvious. Death is sad. The city, if you have not been informed, is lonely at night. In it, other people are mysteriously uninterested in me, which is sad and lonely, for me, and for them, whether or not they know it.

Occasionally I would try to let things go completely, and exert as little control as possible over the language. Those poems were a mess, and I would stare at them afterward with bored incomprehension.

My bedroom on the second floor of that house on School Street tilted alarmingly. A row of poorly sealed windows looked out onto the street and other crooked little houses. In the backyard, a giant morning glory had taken over, and I marveled at how its purple flowers would open in to admit the pollinators, and then close in the afternoon and die. The next day new flowers would do the same thing.

Winter came, and a cold wind constantly blew through the room. Sometimes flakes of snow would somehow appear inside. A ring of frost on the lip of a glass. I was growing more and more frustrated with the destabilizing ease with which I was able to continually write and erase words on a computer. Things were always happening too fast, and changes were getting made and unmade with alarming frequency. The poems, in their clean, professional fonts, looked so much better than they were. More often than not, I couldn't stop myself tinkering long enough to figure out what felt right and true to me. I desperately needed to slow down.

My new existence felt barely tethered. I thought nothing mattered in my life, which I was willing at a moment's notice to alter. This made me careless and cruel. An equivalent lack of responsibility manifested in my writing. I was always recklessly willing to change anything in the poem to make it more musical, more strange, always skating along the edge of irrelevance and complete lack of necessity. While this makes one an awful boyfriend, friend, brother, son, I think it is an excellent place as a young artist to be. It hones one's skill and teaches the line between intuitive meaning and pointless weirdness.

When I gained a small audience of fellow poets in graduate school, who became friends who deeply mattered to me, and became their reader too, something began to change. It would be a long time before I really understood how much these connections mattered, in life and in writing. But their presence affected me deeply, as a writer. Not only was I at last in a place where other people were serious about poetry. I began to think about them while I was writing. I was able to imagine them moving through the poem. I would move things around and imagine what the effect would be on my readers. And I moved through their poems too, marking where I was baffled or uncertain, always considering the possibility that things could be in a different order. On one hand, I felt a growing freedom and understanding of the composition process, which could sometimes become dizzying. On the other, there was the actual, physical presence of readers who gave direction to that freedom.

*

In a desperate attempt to get away from the limits of my own emotions and experiences, I began walking around the quaint little town, along streets canopied by trees full of blossom, in a permanent unhappy daze, gathering lines, transcribing in my notebook whatever I heard in my mind. What I saw became words, not just to describe what I was seeing. I was also collecting stray thoughts, memories, observations, jokes, comments, questions, strange bits of language on signs or the sides of passing trucks; whatever I saw, overheard, thought, with no discrimination. Each house seemed to emanate a friendly, familial light. I told myself I wasn't writing poetry, just lines, most of which were not particularly promising, but I kept collecting.

I didn't realize it at the time, because I was only vaguely familiar with surrealism, but like those misunderstood idealists I was trying to maintain a more or less constant dream state while I was awake, so that many lines would come to me and bridge the gap between reality and the unconscious. I was also obsessed with a particular group of artists, Der Blaue Reiter (The Blue Rider), whose most famous member was Wassily Kandinsky. They operated in the space between figurative art and abstraction, and their gorgeous, colorful canvases shimmered with the twin energies of representation of the world and intimations of all that was beyond mere representations.

I wanted my poems, like those paintings, to reflect and engage with reality while also pointing always to something beyond it, something I did not truly understand or grasp but could feel was there. I desired the simultaneous presence of both worlds, and had no idea how to summon either, much less both. Out of desperation I began setting my alarm earlier and earlier and getting up just to assemble those lines, together with others that I had written earlier and cut out of poems that were not working. Most of the lines were not good. I wasn't sure what to do with them, other than to retype them and try to move them around, again and again, until something felt like a poem.

I signed up for a workshop with James Tate, whom I worshipped. The feeling was not mutual. We both suspected I could not write any good poems, and the evidence appeared weekly. It was early spring and, I remember, very cold. The winter seemed to continue. I brought in poem after poem, and like the weather they just got worse. One week I read with a growing sense of dread as I heard my voice in the room, and Jim looked at me, for what seemed like a very long time. Then, with one hand ceremoniously turning the paper over in the air, he placed it with exaggerated care back on the table, facedown, saying just one word: *No*.

In rearranging these lines, I wasn't writing poems exactly, just trying to connect things from different times I had walked around, collecting, to see what suggested itself. I was looking for anything that meant something. I searched through them for clues or signs, the faint suggestion of a scene or situation.

I did this for many weeks without much success. Then, without warning, I realized that the lines were collecting themselves into a scene, an auditorium when an orchestra is warming up, before the performance. Those disorganized sounds become the real performance, the one that happens before the official one begins. The audience rises and applauds. Guided by something nameless, I kept writing and putting things together with a new instinct, or maybe an old one that had at last emerged. The poem felt in some way both lighter and, for the first time, essential, though (or perhaps because) I couldn't say what I was doing.

I brought the poem to class, but strangely, for the first time, I did not care what anyone said. After I read it, Tate looked up at me, and gave an enigmatic "Huh." Then he spoke for a long time about what he liked. But I did not really listen. I had already learned something about writing poetry, something that could never be forgotten.

*

In that little room overlooking School Street, surrounded by snow, I began to type each version of whatever poem I was writing, over and over again, on the Royal Quiet Deluxe, not quiet at all. Each time when I was done I would yank the poem dramatically out of the platen and stare at it, maybe making some marks. If I wanted to see what the change would look like, I'd have to retype, even if it was just a single word. The process was slow, meditative, hypnotic. I could work for many hours like this. The sound of a typewriter is unmistakable. It resonates in a room, timelessly, through doors, into the world. The sounds entirely dominated my skull. I began not to think about but to hear how necessary each word was or wasn't: if I could skip something to avoid typing it for the fiftieth or hundredth time, and then when I read it, it sounded fine, I would never look back.

I also had a secret, immutable rule. If I ever mistyped a word— *horse* for *house*, *ward* for *word* or *vary* for *very*, *find* for *fine*—I would have to keep it. It was a pact I made with myself, to trust my unconscious, that what seemed to be an error was actually a sign. Occasionally I would accidentally place my fingers on the keys incorrectly and type an unpronounceable word or string of gibberish, which I would then have to try to decipher.

The poems changed, becoming more focused. There are at least fifty, and sometimes several hundred, typewritten versions of each of those poems in boxes somewhere. It was when I came at last upon very simple poems, short ones by Vasko Popa, by Greek poets Yannis Ritsos and C. P. Cavafy, and the Poles Wisława Szymborska and Zbigniew Herbert, that I started to see the possibilities of a simple, clear narrative that allowed for both worldly and dream-like events. I wrote that way for a while, imagining a reader, and being as deliberate as possible. I was also writing for myself, to find out what I would say. I was like a child, finally hearing the stories I had wanted all along.

The combination of gathering lines constantly by hand and returning with them to see what emerged was simultaneously elongated and focused by using the typewriter. Plus it was just fun to pound the keys hard and hear the satisfying clacking sound. I was, at last, *working*.

two sleeps behind me
in the rooms

one a dark tunnel
lit
with the warm yellow glow
conductors guide their passengers by

the other full of terrible cries
the dead and living would make
if science were not a religion

now I am looking at the black leaves
against the black sky
and thinking, later I will go

watch a building being constructed
and hear the machines

make something rise
up toward
the constant death of clouds
whose names I do not know

My Life (Second Draft)

It's early again, and I can hear the train, many miles away, running along the edge of the bay. Since there is no other ambient noise, it is as clear as if it were just down the hill. Until he was born and got older and began to talk all the time about trains, to ask me if I heard that sound, I didn't hear it, though it was there all along. Now it is as if my ear has been tuned to it, no matter how faint the signal.

Two sleeps. The first dark but calm. The second, the sleep of an adult? Is this what Sarah is hearing, deep in sleep? Maybe it is not about her sleep, but about mine. Whose sleep is full of these terrible cries, and who is crying out?

At first the train enters the poem, Then it is taken out, leaving only its echo in "conductor," a word that resonates with other meanings (electrical, musical) potentially to be explored.

The poem is still circling around something important. The objects in it—sleep, tunnel, light and its absence, tree, sky, building, clouds—seem to be holding a place for something I cannot yet clearly understand. Later, through the window of a room in downtown Oakland, I will look up from my reading or writing and become distracted once again by the endlessly fascinating spectacle across the street of a new structure being built, some kind of office building, or apartments. Giant machines lifting huge girders and other things, nameless to me, high in the air.

*

Sometimes he wakes up in the middle of the night. Even if he hardly makes a sound, I wake up too. It must be the legacy of that first night, the connection formed when he slept on my chest. Even through two closed doors I can hear him, tossing restlessly, then murmuring a few words.

When I go in, I ask him what is wrong, already knowing he won't be able to answer me. Standing there in the dark, above his bed, looking down at his small body, I am wracked with anguish. Other parents can talk with their children. A few days ago, I had watched another father, who had been chatting with his four-year-old, a classmate of our son's. I said to that father, You know, I have never had a conversation with my child. At most, a single exchange, one question asked and a short answer. He looked at me in horror, and we both turned away.

Even though he is not feeling well, soon he is happily talking about trains. He loves trains so much and talks about them all the time in his waking life; they must fill his dream life as well. I don't know what it is exactly about trains. Maybe because they are similar enough to belong all to one category, but full of endless variations (diesel, bullet, steam engine, hopper car, gondola car, flat car, tanker, beloved caboose), each with intricate, functional parts. Maybe it is the variegated anthropomorphic faces of the engines: headlights for eyes, rivets for mouth, and sometimes a little chimney hat. They can be endlessly drawn and colored and organized into satisfying rows. There are many mesmerizing videos of people making trains out of recycled household objects, like soda cans and boxes, re-purposing everything into gorgeous models where every part fits gracefully into the next.

I never thought much about trains before. Now I am fascinated by them too. And I realize how many songs there are that I listen to, and sing and play on guitar, that refer to them, their lonesome whistles, their endless, lonely possibility.

Once, I asked him why he loved trains so much, and as an answer received, "Because they run on tracks," which is as good a reason as any. Predictability intersecting with the pleasure of variation. Or just the satisfaction of straight lines and that rhythmic clacking sound.

I listen, because so often in the language he uses, taken from books or television shows, there is a key to how he is feeling. I have learned his choices are never random. A train has broken down; the tunnel is blocked. It needs help, to be fixed. It has overheated; it needs water. I feel certain he must be getting sick. I touch his forehead, which is still cool, and go back into our bedroom, though I know I won't fall asleep again, at least not until it is close to morning.

I can't sleep, so I step out into the night. The air is barely breathable, but I look up for a moment at the moon. One of the freight trains is blowing its horn down the hill, through the night silence sounding far closer than it is.

*

I've made a playlist of songs about trains he and I listen to, including many by Johnny Cash, who I am proud to say is his favorite. "Blue Train," "Train of Love," Train, train, train, I've got a thing about trains. But the song he loves most of all is by Elizabeth Cotten, "Freight Train." Many have tried to master the way she keeps the rhythm by plucking the top strings with the thumb of her right hand, while the fingers on that same hand pick out the melody on the other strings. It's one of the first songs I remember my dad teaching me how to play on guitar.

Cotten wrote "Freight Train" when she was thirteen years old. Then she got married and completely stopped playing music.

After her daughter got older and moved away, Cotten left her husband and began going back and forth between North Carolina and Washington, D.C. She took various temporary jobs there, including one in a department store. One day she found a little girl wandering around in the store, and brought her back to her frantic mother. It turned out the little girl was Peggy Seeger, sister of Pete. Cotten became a part-time nanny to the Seeger family.

One day Cotten picked up the guitar and began playing music to the children. She taught them "Freight Train," which Peggy learned and then played to others. Through Seeger family performances, the song became a folk music hit.

I had a vague memory of this story, and once looked it up. I was startled to discover that the Seeger (oddly similar to my mother's maiden name, Seiger) family had lived in the very town in Maryland I grew up in (which, yes, really is called Chevy Chase). In fact, the Seegers lived one mere block away, what I grew up calling "catty corner," across Connecticut Avenue. The Seeger family was gone by the time we moved there in the early 1970s. But it is odd to think that I was learning to finger-pick "Freight Train" in the Libba Cotten style from my father not a three-minute walk away from where the song had been rediscovered. I feel an instant of dizziness at the barely avoided fate of that song, nearly lost forever. What other songs have we never heard?

I play "Freight Train" for him practically every day, on insistent request, the same intricate interplay between right and left hand, every finger doing something different in a way that works only if you don't think about it. The tune is both happy and melancholic. The lyrics are specific and symbolic, full of resigned despair at being so proximate to the possibility of escape without ever being able to enact it:

When I die, oh bury me deep
Down at the end of old Chestnut Street
So I can hear old Number Nine
As she comes rolling by

When I die, oh bury me deep
Down at the end of old Chestnut Street
Place the stones at my head and feet
And tell them all I've gone to sleep

I have tried to teach him to sing alternate lyrics, because it frightens me to hear him singing about death. But he's a traditionalist.

I stand on the sidewalk and look at the moon, huge and red through the haze. I feel a deep, ancient terror at being outside the house with my wife and my sleeping son inside, so I only stay out for a moment, then, like a father, go back inside.

*

Inside, Sarah is already asleep. I knew something about her as soon as we met. She was not only brilliant and beautiful and kind. I could sense in her a deep honesty and directness, an inability to lie to herself or anyone.

I asked her to marry me after we were together for only a year. It was very romantic, we were in Paris, where I was teaching for the summer. I bought a not-too-expensive ring and gave it to her in her favorite place in the city, a park with a secret door. She said, I don't know yet. I was stunned, hurt, and full of admiration.

With every change, from getting married to having a child, I wanted to move forward immediately, and she agonized. I always dismissed her concerns. And then, once we discovered that our path with our child was going to be so different from everything we had taken for granted, I fell apart. She did too, while also getting stronger. I wanted a parent to come along and relieve me of all this responsibility and tell me the fairy tale that everything, no matter what, will be all right. Long before I did, she saw what a tremendous, necessary act of sustained will it would take for us to let go of our suburban, bourgeois programming, even though all it had gotten us was anxiety and unhappiness. She stopped wanting that long before I did, and began to see our son clearly for who he was, which was the first step toward realizing that our lives are the treasure we already have.

There are alarming statistics about couples who go through what we were going through, and I can see why. Everything is impossibly charged, and the whole marriage becomes a site for anxiety. There are constant opportunities to let each other down, and the isolation becomes overwhelming. I've learned to hold some things back, not to depend on her every time I feel a desperate need for certainty that no one can provide.

The instinct to preserve what is between us has strengthened me and my courage to sit with my own terror. Sometimes I feel some calm. Our little family has grown impossibly precious to me in its weird difference. I can no longer imagine it any other way. Sometimes, when I talk with another child or observe a family up close, I see how different we are, and that terror returns. Then I look at her and see her strength, how much farther she is ahead of me in seeing what is true, that each life and each story is different, that everyone has difficulties, that we have been given the gift of awareness.

I MET MY WIFE

I met my wife
in a bar
you could throw
a Frisbee from
and hit Emily
Dickinson's grave
which would be
uncool and not.
Until that night
my whole life
had been a conference
where voices
amiably disagreed
until paralysis ensued.
When I looked
in her face
something actually
for the first time
spoke saying
Home is where
you've never lived,
not yet.
What else.
Before she said it
I knew her Old
Testament name.
Home as everyone
knows is hard,
in each room
the most terrible
moments keep
lasting, obscure
green velvet
continual past
light from under

every doorway
pours into
the hallway,
you are drawn
to enter and fear.
It's horrible
and good to go
through each door
into every room,
to keep standing
in that green light,
to spread your arms
and take it
into your fur,
no fantasy
is ever better,
still alive you
open your eyes
and go back down
the stairs to find
the other
in the kitchen
stirring something,
someone says
have a cookie,
it won't kill you.

A few months ago, a dad and I were leaning over a fence, watching our kids play in the yard after school. Improbably, he had been a fighter pilot in a foreign army before he immigrated here to work in "business." He clearly adores his daughter, who never stops talking. For a moment, a friendship seems possible. The dads will do dad-type activities together in which the kids can participate in happy, mutual edification. Maybe they would be a good fit, the chatty, bossy girl and the sweet-natured, quieter boy, while the dads in varying states of ruggedness discuss the fate of the world, and sports.

My son was playing by himself, making a multicolored train out of large plastic blocks, singing. Living with him can feel like moving through a series of books, songs, shows, scenarios, in which he will happily exist, while also being happy to have others participate by playing another character or singing along. From the outside it looks like he is unaware, but he is actually absorbing much of what is going on around him, at least the parts that interest him. In a risky moment of openness I said to the other dad, "You know, sometimes I look at my kid and think . . ." I'm not sure how I was going to finish the thought. Maybe with something about difference, and how fear of it is conventional and shows no imagination. But the girl's father completed the sentence: "That something in him is missing?"

I felt a familiar tiredness. I did not want to explain. There is a brightness in my son's eyes, a force of life radiating from him, that is obvious to anyone who comes to him without presupposition. But the word *autism* has a talismanic, totalizing power. Some misinformed parents would even expose their children to diseases, forgoing the protection of vaccines, rather than chance that this word will end up connected to their name. I can see that fear flicker in the eyes of the fathers, the mothers. There but for the grace of heretofore untestable genetics go we.

*

Today when we went outside, Sarah wore a mask, which I was skeptical about until I pretty much immediately felt a burning in the back of my throat, and in my lungs. We drove the ten minutes or so to the preschool. His three teachers are so kind and loving with him. They look like they could be in an excellent indie band from the 1990s, before everyone had stylists. Lots of tattoos and vintage dresses.

They talk about how much progress he is making, about how he is working on his language, about how the aide who goes to school with him helps him engage in "social games," so he can practice interacting with other kids, which he would not do of his own volition. They talk about how the other kids ask about him on the days he is not there. They talk about his joy. They talk about how hard it is for him to enter play, because children are unpredictable, and how his aide is so good at creating situations where that can happen, so he can practice and gain confidence, incrementally. They tell us that he no longer avoids the other children, but watches them play with pleasure and affection and occasionally tries without any encouragement or overt preparation to play with them himself, that he is focusing for so much longer when he does art and other activities. He used to not be able to sit still for longer than literally five seconds, and now it is a long time that he can be absorbed in making something. I know what they mean. I love watching him that way, I can in those moments see in his face the person whom he will become.

There is much talk of "progress" and "promise." He is clever, quick, growing and learning and absorbing and developing new skills all the time. He is bright and funny and sweet and happy. He loves school. He has a stunning capacity for memory. He loves music and sings melodies back perfectly after hearing them only once.

All this talk about progress of course depends on the underlying, unspoken, undeniable fact of his difference. There is no way that these teachers are talking to other parents the way they do to us. Whatever those kids are working on is in the context of "normal" development. His development is taking place on a different track, and to get him to do many of the essential things that come naturally to other children requires great effort and patience and skill. He "learns differently," as the kindly (they are all kindly) curly-haired teacher with the cat glasses and two sleeves of tattoos (they all have tattoos) casually reminds us. We have not forgotten. Those are the sorts of accurate gentle phrases that strike terror into the heart of this suburban, test-taking, competitive overachiever, one who has always been sure that no matter what, some internal intelligence will guide him forward in any situation, in any room.

*

When he was diagnosed, shortly after he turned two, I had no idea what being on the autism spectrum meant. All I knew about was *Rain Man* and kids who didn't speak to anyone and threw huge tantrums whenever things didn't go precisely their way, kids who were strange and friendless and didn't play sports or join clubs or go to the best colleges, or to college at all. Maybe they couldn't even live on their own. Kids with "special needs" who were always in different classrooms. Sometimes you might see them in the halls. I thought if you were autistic you didn't have feelings like "normal people," which is, it turns out, completely wrong, along with almost everything else I thought I knew.

I felt that suddenly all my dreams for him were over. That the whole trajectory of his life, and ours, had been fundamentally altered. That we were exiled from the normal world, subject from now on to pity and special treatment. It is so painful and shameful to write these things. I'm not sure I can ever publish them, because I don't want him ever to think for a moment that he or his life seemed insufficient to me, or scared me. But the truth is, I was very afraid, and sometimes still am, though of what I am honestly not sure.

One of the things that is hard is a feeling of isolation, especially from other parents. I feel like I am trying to justify who he is, or prove somehow through my explanations that he is just as good as other people, and to communicate through the positive nature of my descriptions that I am okay, that he is okay, that everything is going to be okay. I resist the urge to say several times that he is smart, that he has no cognitive impairment and in fact is quite intelligent, that he is bright, so many different words for the same need for him to be seen in a certain way, as I was seen, and needed to be.

I despise that feeling in me of desperation, that need to be seen a certain way. So more and more I have chosen to be silent about his differences. When writing or talking about him I feel like I am constantly in danger of narrowing him as a person through how I write, overly defining him. But I want to keep trying to understand. The only way I can is through writing.

*

Maybe the point of writing through these feelings here, and in poems, is not to capture him in words, or to present him to anyone, but to record the ongoing experience of being alive in relation to difficulty, which is really the situation we are all in, whether or not we acknowledge it. Maybe it is to truly consider the nature of a spectrum, not just in relation to my son but in all aspects of life and artistic practice. I fear drifting into banality and a different sort of falseness, this time of comfort. Yet writing these words I feel absolutely sure that I need to love and accept and see the great variety of being and not be so narrow. I know this is true, and that the path to not just loving but fully accepting my son and other people who are different is what will ultimately lead me to such love of myself, and of Sarah. And surely instead of being afraid, I could be asking better questions, of myself and of the world that surrounds my son, even if no immediate answers are forthcoming.

In the end I have the distinct sense that so much of this comes down to language. I am so conditioned to think of intelligence as equivalent to facility with language and conceptual thinking: the ability to organize and synthesize ideas and return them to the world in an attractive package, the quicker the better. But what if this is not the most important thing? Every time I turn on my computer and connect to the swirl of online conversation, I am confronted with endless variations of this, manifested as content. Is it helping? Or is it just the endless churn of blathering language that does nothing to solve any of our problems, to truly educate anyone or help anyone think in new and creative ways?

In what ways can someone think that have nothing to do with language at all? What about pictures? Music? A whole emotional life taking place in a brain that does not immediately default to jabbering away about itself, with that hunger to be seen and admired?

Of course I want to talk to him, and to know what he thinks about things. But just because I don't know doesn't mean he isn't thinking. I see him passionately engaged, or sometimes listening very carefully to music or something I can't hear, or looking intently at something I can't see.

Sometimes, like tonight, he is in the mood to talk. I noticed that he was having little conversations with us, which is a big deal for him. Without any fanfare (what's fanfare?) he has started asking us questions and, when we answer, following up, things having to do with play, dinner, plans, and so on. It could almost pass unnoticed except that these are the basic building blocks of human interaction, the emergence of which we have been praying for, for years. When Sarah was done singing him his songs, he asked for daddy songs, and she said, "I don't know, I'll check and see if he's available." And he said, "Is Daddy coming? Is he coming?" All these natural things that other parents take for granted, and then when he starts to do them, it's a miracle.

*

The word *autism* causes a lot of uninformed fear. When I heard that word, I too was deathly afraid. I thought I knew what it meant. I had seen all those movies. I suddenly saw my son in a certain way, the present and future closed down. It shames me now to think how, before I met my son, I walked through the world. That word erased difference, variation, and possibility. My so-called knowledge shadowed the world. I had to unlearn that word.

Of such linguistic reductions I have learned, necessarily, to be rightly wary. When I read what I have written about my son above, it seems clearly true, but also hardly even a fraction of the story. It's not him, not even close to being him, which raises the question: What is the point of writing about him at all, and how can I reconcile this desire to understand more about him, and myself, through writing, and also be the father I want so much to be?

I want in my poems, as in life, always to see my son. So in them I never write *autism*, not out of shame or because I don't think it is real, nor to be elusive or mysterious, but for the opposite reason. Its meaning, its sound, blocks out all individuality and actuality. The pushing away of that word is not a denial, but the creating of a space so I and everyone else can truly encounter my son, just as we should encounter everyone.

Through a painful, necessary process, I have begun to perceive what I never could have before. Often it is overwhelming. When I walk past people in the store, on the street, in an airport, I feel and see each life, each in its difference, its limitation, and instead of turning away, I want to learn to embrace everyone. Audre Lorde writes:

> I urge each one of us here to reach down into that deep
> place of knowledge inside herself and touch that terror

and loathing of any difference that lives there. See whose face it wears.

Each time I read her words, I think about how my own easy liberalism for so long smugly masked an intensely hierarchical and judgmental attitude toward anyone I did not perceive as gifted, smart, quick, cultured. This judgment was, of course, ultimately directed toward myself, as I constantly fell short of my own impossible ideals.

I have for my whole life misunderstood difference. I thought difference from the ideal was a mortal flaw, something to be fixed, or hidden, or despised. I turned that outward and inward. Now, as a father, I must reach down into myself and touch the terror of difference, which is of course my own, the terror and the difference. Both wear my own face. There is something past that fear: the possibility of acceptance, which in turn opens up the possibility of love. My love draws me onward. Yet the most painful thing for me to admit is that my own fear still so often overtakes me. The struggle is in the poems, and I write them to stay awake, to remember.

*

"Everyone who is born," writes Susan Sontag, "holds dual citizenship, in the kingdom of the well and the kingdom of the sick." I had found this out once before, once removed, when my father became suddenly ill with a brain tumor and died. Now I was finding it out in a different way. We had walked into that office in Berkeley in one story, and walked out in another, in the cloud of some diagnosis, inside a new life.

For my whole life I believed, unthinkingly, that I was normal. Language, especially, had always been where I was not only most normal, but meritoriously exceptional. Now, at last, I didn't know what to say, not just for a day (as when I put my head down and wept at the sight of my father's pine coffin, and would not greet anyone at the funeral or grave), but for months. Every interaction, except with my wife and son, felt fraught, and false. There was too much to explain, and I didn't have the words. All my language about my child felt partial, contaminated by my ignorance. I knew there was so much to understand, and that I was going to have to change to even begin to speak authentically.

Every moment of speech outside my controlled environment felt dangerous. It is truly staggering how often people make jokes about autism, and how behavior that is not "normal" is often mockingly attributed to that difference. Some of my closest friends often made such remarks and jokes, even those who know our family and my son. Worst of all, to my absolute despair, I realized that I myself, out of ignorance and a false, smug sense of security in my own centrality, surely had in the past made those same jokes too, a horror that to this day keeps me awake, in shame and sorrow.

I had never given disability any serious thought. I believed what I was told: that if you were disabled, you deserved compassion, accommodation, pity. You were not "normal," which of course was not your fault, but in the end, you should not get in the way of progress, achievement, education, success. Even typing these words makes me feel ill, but they are the truth.

Because of the nature of my son's difference, so much of my radical rethinking was around ideas of language. Not just how my son was learning to speak, but also how I was learning to speak authentically, respectfully, accurately, about my son, and about so many others whose experience I had, up until then, not considered. How do our everyday speech acts, and our writing, create the world we are living in? If we don't like that world, what can we do to change it?

I think of the government buildings I remember from childhood in Washington, D.C., the massive Departments of State, Treasury, Interior, the huge monuments to Lincoln and Jefferson, the Capitol building. I remember staring at their endless steps upward. Now, I am sure, they have ramps, but they did not always. If one is in a wheelchair, and there is no ramp, there is no way in. The building is not accessible. Who is responsible? I was just beginning to learn, at last, that disability is a problem with the world. The world is built, literally and figuratively, in a certain way, to serve certain people, who are "normal" in mind and in body. But what if this normality is merely a construction convenient for the so-called normal, and inimical to everyone else?

*

Sarah and I walk into a new conference room, paid for, presumably, by insurance money. Autism, as I have come to understand, is a big new business opportunity, and small companies that were once nonprofits, maybe started by parents of autistic children or dedicated therapists, are being bought up by big corporations. The therapy company we worked with since our son was two was recently bought in such a transaction, and the founder, who came into the office a few days during the Christmas holiday to play with our child for hours and encourage us about his joyful intelligence and potential, was forced out. Now there are many new systems and protocols and forms. More important, a quality of kindness, of respect for difference, of valuing atypical ways of being along with gently and respectfully helping children learn to adjust to challenging situations as much as possible, seems to have dissipated.

We stare at an expensive wall-sized screen as a supervisor describes to us all the ways our child deviates from "normal" development, and gives us a plan to bring him closer to that norm.

If we don't do these things, we are told, he is likely not to "make progress," and if he doesn't "make progress," he will no longer be eligible for therapy. A special late-capitalist form of Kafkaesque reasoning. All their kind words about neurodiversity dissolve into plans for improvement. Perhaps they are being kind and thoughtful and caring, and I am only hearing it this way because of my own relentless indoctrination in the cult of normality. We walk out of the room, into the bright corporate light, exhausted and demoralized. Something has gone very wrong, and I start to feel certain we are no longer helping him.

Our job is to teach him that his job is to learn to meet the world, but not to submit to it. To support him as he moves through the world in his own way, growing and changing and adapting at his own pace, like everyone. And our job is to change not him, but the world.

*

Paul Valéry wrote:

> A fine line of poetry is a fruit plucked from the tree. But which tree? This leads to the curious point of trying to *make* the tree whose fruit would be this fruit. Finally, then, it is the fruit of two trees. One hidden, unknowable, which produced the fruit. The other, the work in which the fruit takes a more or less necessary place.

According to Wikipedia, to form a fruit, one tree sends the pollen out, it drifts until it finds the other. Some trees do self-pollinate, it is true, but those trees grow less fruit. Sometimes Wikipedia is as beautiful as any poem: "The pollination process requires a carrier for the pollen, which can be animal, wind, or human intervention."

You have been given the line, the image, the idea. Like a child or a new love, it is never what you expected. It wants you to change your life. You hear the line. It comes from somewhere. You've gathered, or maybe fathered, it. It comes to you or you to it. No one can tell you how it happens. Sometimes you write for a while, feeling nothing, until, almost unnoticed, something starts with mysterious life to glow.

You feel yourself resist its strangeness. What does it mean? Is that what I meant to say? What do you do with it then? You cannot turn away.

Make somewhere for it to live and belong. It is your job to imagine and invent that tree on which the treasured fruit could happily thrive. The strange treasure of a line, or image, or symbol, or word, or thought, or moment, needs the poem so that it can be more than itself in isolation, so that it can be truly perceived.

Try to remember. The whole point of writing that first draft is just to hear the music, and then once you hear the music, you look for what could contain it. Reverse engineering. Farewell, old tree. Hello, something else, from which can hang the music you have found.

Try to be quiet for once, to listen for something you love. Let it come to you. Then build a structure in which what you love—a line, an image, a word—can exist: a situation, a scene, a sonnet, a ghazal, an ode, an abandoned palace, a happy graveyard, a breeze, a ghost ship's wake, a map in winter, a rose factory, someone crossing the ocean in a fabulously unseaworthy craft, a marriage, a meal, a crucial childhood memory that never occurred, a radio being endlessly, impatiently tuned, so on and so on and so on until the line can live there. You hear them. Then the poem can begin.

*

I wrote a poem quickly one morning that frightened me. I thought, I can never publish this. Reading the poem aloud to myself in my room, it felt too raw, and personal, not just about me, but about the experiences Sarah was having too (at least as I understood them). It was completely honest about something very private, in a certain way, at a moment of extreme duress.

Virginia Woolf wrote:

> The impact of poetry is so hard and direct that for the moment there is no other sensation except that of the poem itself. What profound depths we visit then—how sudden and complete is our immersion! There is nothing here to catch hold of; nothing to stay us in our flight.

Whenever I write about my son, I hear and feel the terrifying immanence of poetry, its potential to crystallize a moment of feeling with intolerable power. I suddenly find myself dangerously close to primal feelings I would otherwise call, imprecisely and with a certain degree of safe distance, love and fear. Those words are too big to truly feel. For me, they can be felt only as they take shape in poems.

Yet, that power of the lyric—its presence and actuality in the moment—can be its limitation. Each time I write about my son, I am intensely pained by an idea, that anyone would think that what I am feeling in one poem would be the totality of my experience. The struggle, the experience, is the poems. Part of that experience is fear: of what it means to be different in a highly conformist society constructed for the benefit of people with certain kinds of skills and minds. But there are so many other wonderful things, like watching a singular child who is loving and kind and good-natured and bright and affectionate grow in his own ways, many of them different from what anyone expected, marvelous therefore and nonetheless.

I think, I should bury the poems. I should hide them, so no one can see me, or him, or my fears, my uncertainty, my desperate love. What if I reveal not enough about who he is, my admiration for him, my love of his qualities, my hopes, my own crucial process of change? What if he reads this someday and feels I was not proud? That those moments of fear and despair are, however understandable, failures, and that the best part of me is the part that looks at myself and the world and perceives these differences as our greatest glory?

At the same time, I have never felt more sure of the personal necessity of writing the lyric. Many days it is my only relief from the endless circling of worry, the futile speculations. I also know that my life with my wife and son has become my story, and therefore my subject. I could not continue to be a writer and not try to write through my feelings, as they cycle and contradict each other and change.

I often think the same thing about this prose book. Sometimes I write things that terrify me in their directness about my confusion, my fear, my shame. Sometimes no matter how hard I search for some clarity, in my feelings about my son, about the world, only further questions come.

In this poem, I wrote, without thinking, "he is my painful joy," a difficult line for me to accept. But it's true. This is exactly how I feel. But only sometimes. It is, in the poems, what I continually rediscover, this feeling of paradox in my experience, and in the experience, I strongly suspect, of all parenting. Is this what is hidden, what we can't speak about or permit ourselves to feel? What is hidden to all parents? To anyone in a relationship? To anyone alive? Can't poems ask the sorts of questions no other writing can? I have thought about that so much, and also about how, for me, when it comes to my son, to my life, it is not enough to write poems, which are, as Woolf points out, so sudden. I was told once by a fellow parent of a neurodivergent child to add to every negative sentence a single word: *yet*. She can't do *x*, yet. A linguistic imposition of a hope that reflects the reality, that things are always changing.

Especially in poems, temporality can be a prison, and I can feel I am caging both myself and my son inside certain moments of my own fear. This is why I am sure I need both poetry and prose. This is the real purpose of this writing: to write into and through these matters, out of them and back again, continually clarifying the questions so that I can understand them in a way that I cannot through poetry alone. I needed a new form, poetry entwined with prose in the middle of their own making.

In my loneliness and confusion and fear, I know I need to connect to others, to strangers. To cross, however uncertainly, the distance between what I think and feel, and you, mysterious reader. Adrienne Rich: "Poetry can break isolation, show us to ourselves when we are outlawed or made invisible, remind us of beauty where no beauty seems possible, remind us of kinship where all is represented as separation."

MY LIFE

four years ago
on Martin Luther King day
in the afternoon
the little strip
said it was time,
so we did it twice
laughing through
that grim comical
despair familiar
to all modern
conceivers,
it was magical
only that it worked

but now I know
it was then
my life began,
we made so
many plans
circumstances
already waited
to obviate,
suddenly he was born,
a room full of blood
and shouting,
he stayed calm
sleeping on my chest
a long time while
they sewed you up,
he and I
in a room alone
under a soft white light,
one nurse came
to say it was all right,
you were not
but you were there,
I talked to him,
whatever I said
I don't remember,
then came the proud
sleepless happy
sorrow months
then slow realizing
playground dread,
the year
of diagnosis when
our life kept
being a place
for worsening fears
in enviable comfort
to occur as we

graciously received
the humiliation
of being the ones
gratefully not to be,
those many hours
in the bedroom screaming
then lurching out
for exhausted walks,
trying with no
success to protect
us from everything
anyone could say,
gradually all our friends
and family lovingly
without intention
back into their lives
abandoned us,
we did not know
it was just us
growing stronger
in relation to a future
where no one
without permission
may join us,
now we're moving
fortunate ones
from our beloved house
to another on a hill
near a school
where his mind
happily alive
in music can grow,
can I say he is
my painful joy,
he thinks
in rhyme,
the truest friend

to no one yet
he is my
favorite word
remembrancer,
why am I telling you
you know it all
and yet to say
my version
of our story
in the morning
very early
imagining you
sitting behind me
touching my shoulder
scares and
comforts me,
before I go
I want to tell you
something new,
all the time
I walk around
thinking this life
yes but is this lovely
accident correct
and someday
how will it happen
to our bodies
and when it does
will we feel
like we lived or
just lived through

(from *Father's Day*)

TWO SLEEPS

black leaves
against the black sky
no need to say
what we've learned
we know:
the best minds
have invented t
terrible machines
to ask new questions
how many
metal trees
will it take
to reverse the past
should we plant
them in the desert
where only
spirits go?
you want to change
I tell myself
so if you hear
that old tired
despair song
go tell
the black sky
full of smoke
it will not listen
if I am still
then more still
I can feel
two sleeps
in the rooms
behind me
clouds of breath
it's getting lighter
soon the kids
underneath thenwindow
will pass
their voices seem
to live on
long after
they have carried
their worries
up the hill

if I lidten
I can hear
their thoughts
small fears
cover over
what they do not
know they know:
the death system
has already decided
our fate
their fate
after they pass
the traffic sounds
like a train
under the sea
like t he constant
black tunnel
I enter fearing
my son won't go
up the hill
with them then
bey ond the city
I like to imagine
I am watching
a building rise
up toward
the constant death
of the clouds
whose names
I do not know

All the World (Third Draft)

It's so smoky and we have nothing to do, so I put him in the car and we drive through his favorite tunnel. This gives him immense joy. We don't need a destination. Together we sing in the car, train songs, Beatles songs, Guided by Voices. Lizzo. Today, through the smoke, we drive through the tunnel, back and forth. I have through his excitement come to love when it suddenly gets dark and everything focuses down, the sound and the headlights.

In the poem "Two Sleeps," the tunnel has become my own worry, something I go inside again and again, not really believing I will emerge. The lines that began the poem have now become the title, and the poem is more directly about the current oppressive atmospheric conditions. One sign that a draft is struggling is when it bounces around among various pronouns. The scope of earlier drafts was more narrowly focused on my own circumstances, the three of us. In this draft, an unspecified collective first person has appeared, but the poem also seems interested in the experiences of the individual. It's not clear what the relationship between those perspectives is, much less exactly who this "we" is.

The poem has also introduced a "they," the kids walking past our house. We live on a hill that leads up to the elementary, middle, and high schools. A lot of kids walk past in the mornings, and I hear them talking and shouting. I suspect they are filled with the usual social and academic worries that seem so large and important at that age. Yet it's hard not to think about how they must feel a deeper dread. And it's hard too not to wonder whether my kid will, when he is old enough, be among them, or if he is headed in a different direction.

So there is a lot going on, and the poem seems right now mostly to be a place where potentially conflicting ideas can be held and considered later. There are a lot of other problems with this current draft too. It's too breathy. The beginning isn't really very compelling, and the title is just a placeholder, because the subject of the poem has not revealed itself. There are various moments of uninteresting slippage in the poem, and other times when it feels heavy-handed and obvious.

There has to be something that feels—can I say truthful?—about the connections. If the connections and movement of the poem have no necessity or momentum, the poem is dead on the page in a different way. Sometimes there is a danger in mechanisms of language themselves, which can lead poets to make links that have only the semblance of necessity. For instance, it is all too easy to use *like*. The dreaded weak simile. In the current draft, the imaginative work to truly connect the elements of the poem has not yet been done. Like a train, like a tunnel, like I am watching. All those *like*s must be removed, and I have to ask myself: Are things really, truly similar? And if so, how? And what does it mean? When similes merely elaborate, it can spoil the effect of what has just been said, which is almost always more resonant if you leave it alone, with a little silence trailing after.

I probably overdid it with the lines "the death system / has already decided / their fate." But not by much. And I have the sense that the end is too close to something I've written before. I know I just have to keep pushing and pushing the thought forward, always with the sense that most of what I am thinking/writing is not interesting, not moving in an interestingly necessary way. But I just keep throwing things down, following along, even though I know it is not happening.

For me, so much of making poems is fitting things together. Finding a click that feels like it taps into a deeper meaning. Sometimes it can happen very easily, and instinctively. And that instinct can be correct. But if, after the initial excitement of making something, it turns out no real connection is made, and there is no true discovery, if those disparate elements do not truly belong together, it is painfully dissatisfying.

*

Each time I sit down to write a poem, I don't know what I am doing. Even after all these years, this can still be uncomfortable. I was trained practically from birth to succeed, to know what I am doing, to have plans and goals and to achieve whatever it is I set out to do. It is difficult to hold inside myself the idea that the only way to find out what I really need to say is to let go, which I never really know exactly how to do.

Sometimes it can help to have a loose idea of what I want to write "about," though from experience I have come to realize this is certain to change. Often it's just a desire to see what happens if I start playing around with a certain word, what sorts of things will come up. It's probably more than anything just about as incautious and idea-less as groping in the dark with a paper clip, looking to stick it into an electrical outlet.

Desperately, still, each time I search in books, memories, dreams, dictionaries, conversations, the natural world, anywhere there is either actual language or the possibility of language being generated by experience. The more open I am to those experiences the better. A lot of the way I work in writing poems is to select words, images, phrases, ideas, and so forth through intuition, and then to start to construct something from those selections. Sound is a huge guiding force, though not in any systematic way. It's just part of the attraction I feel, an attraction that sometimes becomes atavistic but, if it survives through the composition process, reveals itself as significant.

Put the headlamp on, I found myself one day saying to my students. Go down into the fearful dark, search for some glow. Grab it, and bring it back up. Then, unlike the miner, instead of turning it over to some gemologist, clear off the debris yourself. Do whatever is necessary to make it ready. Be your own jeweler. Set it, through trial and error, into the proper structure, where it can be seen. The ultimate purpose is not to alter the treasure, but to put it into the world so it can be marveled at, not as something you made, but as something you discovered, that belongs to all of us.

Not too long ago I accidentally came across a short essay by André Breton, the founder of surrealism, in which he writes:

> Therefore, I have always cherished dearly those sentences or fragments of sentences—snippets of monologues or dialogues extracted from dreams and captured with accuracy, both in their articulation and intonation—which remain absolutely clear upon waking. . . . . On every possible occasion, and no matter how sibylline they are, I have collected them with the same care I would precious stones. At one time I would insert them uncut into the beginning of a text. Then I would force myself to "enchain" from there, even if in a very different register, to make certain that what followed held close to them and shared their high degree of effervescence.

I was startled to see what should not have surprised me: that my idea about the jeweler was not new. Later Breton calls the voice that speaks the "shadow mouth." The fragments he hears are "sibyl-line"—mysterious, oracular, and in need of contextualization. The poem is the place where the energy and mysterious knowledge of those gathered phrases can be preserved, held and made visible, enchained to each other and to the world.

The jewel of the particular shining in the gold of the universal is where poetry resides. "Dear reader, I am trying to pry open your casket / with this burning snowflake," writes the great James Tate. I am trying to pry open yours, and mine.

*

There is something about the poem I cannot yet write. Perhaps the pressure of the real is just too great. Like everyone I know, I can't seem to tear myself from social media, the posts about the floods, the government, the camps, the climate. Zero willpower in relation to the minor temptation of technological distraction, the constant ding of something has arrived, let's see what, maybe a prize, maybe despair. Let's look at Twitter and Facebook. I'm sure there is a lot of super-accurate, objective information to be found there, where every secret, however boring or shameful, is confessed.

The sad little dopamine lures of email and the internet, and now social media, have chipped away what surely would add up to a truly horrifying abyss of hours. People my age—that is, of the generation known as X—are the most vulnerable, because we grew up without any access to the internet, then suddenly had it when we were too old for any adult guidance and had a lethal amount of unsupervised time. We have just enough comfort and facility with computers to render ourselves the perfect victims, without any of the self-awareness. We didn't want to give our lives over to "the man," whoever he was. It turns out we were looking for danger in the wrong direction.

I feel so utterly oppressed by the virulence of everyone's certainty, especially my own. I forget how to ask a question. To ask a question, so impossible, changes one's orientation toward the world. And to write a poem is to ask a question. The question only gradually comes into being as the poem moves from chaos to necessity. I depend on my own fragile discipline to refrain from looking at social media, which constantly dismays me, especially in how it manages to convert everything, even questions, into assertions.

Who is listening? What might they need? Which part of the so much I do not yet know am I searching for now? What is this nameless compulsion, and how can it be given a form that does not diminish or falsify it? What can I do in this space that I cannot do anywhere else? What do I think I know that causes me and others grief and harm? How do I need to change in order to survive? What use can I be?

It is difficult to imagine genuine questions in political spaces and social media, or that genuine dialogue will occur. Most of the poems I love to read and reread don't give me conclusive answers to anything, at least not answers they already know. Often what they clarify is painful and reveals irresolvable conflicts, or maybe something that is joyful but also shattered with mortality. Even though a poem is in a certain way unidirectional speech, it can be a singular place to ask real questions, to clarify them and be in them with the reader. Maybe this is a better way forward than preaching to the converted or yelling at those who will never listen.

As a poem moves along, it can begin not merely to answer questions, but to ask deeper, unanswerable ones. The poem becomes a place to eternally preserve the living question. I was going to say in amber, but that is a bad analogy, because the thing preserved in amber has died, and the question is living, so maybe the question is more like a little world, and the poem is its atmosphere.

Sometimes, though, you need to put the poem away, if you are not yet ready to write it. My friends and I have a term for it, which we use to remind each other when we are frustrated with something and need to let it go for a while: "Put it in the drawer." Move on to something else.

*

If you had asked me when I first started writing poems what my religion was, I would have answered, only partially joking, negative capability. That's a phrase John Keats wrote in a letter to his brothers at the end of 1817, from London. He was twenty-two. He writes about his life, what paintings he is seeing, what he is reading, and who he is hanging out with, including famous poets like Wordsworth and Coleridge. And, as he often does in his letters, he digresses to casually confabulate little jeweled observations about literature and creativity.

Keats's famous (among poets) formulation is that in order to write poetry, you have to learn to be, like Shakespeare, "capable of being in uncertainties, mysteries, doubts, without any irritable reaching after fact and reason." I first read about it twenty-five years ago, when I was just starting to write poetry, in Berkeley, as a graduate student: it struck me like a bolt of truth amid all the literary theory and scholarship I was struggling through and already distancing myself from in preparation to go write poetry.

It does not seem too extreme to me to say that it was when I read about negative capability that I started to become a poet. I wasn't one yet, and wouldn't be for a while. But it felt like the idea I had been waiting for my whole life. If I were forced to make a social justification for poetry, I would probably say something about how it keeps language, and therefore a part of us, alive and free. Or how it connects us in a direct, electric, unmediated way that can tap into vast, hidden reservoirs of empathy. But I also think it has something to do with this ability to hold more than one idea at once in the mind. Negative capability is the opposite of our current discourse. It is not how people think on social media, on cable news, on podcasts about politics.

The most famous sentence of Keats's letter is the one I just quoted. But equally important to me is when he writes that the flawed genius Samuel Taylor Coleridge "would let go by a fine isolated verisimilitude caught from the Penetralium of mystery, from being incapable of remaining content with half knowledge." Coleridge would, in other words, take things that were beautiful out of the poem because they didn't fit. He slaughtered his little darlings. I don't know if that's really true. Coleridge actually has a lot of fine isolated verisimilitudes in his poems. The Frost performs its secret ministry. I would build that dome in air. Ye lightnings, the dread arrows of the clouds!

I have heard in many workshops that one should slaughter one's darlings. This is said with such laughter, as if the thing we should be most suspicious of, at least until we are certified masters, is our own love. They say, Kill the lines you love the most. Probably the opposite is the best advice for poetry. Be willing to burn everything else, and keep the lines you love without reason, and rebuild a world for them to live in.

After a long time of writing, I came to understand that for me, the purpose of writing poetry was (and still is) to grope toward these moments of fine isolated verisimilitude, not because they are merely pretty but because they contain something revelatory and true, beautiful as in sublime. To discover those moments, for me, became the only reason to write. Sometimes what I found felt strange. I could not explain why it glowed. If asked, I would lapse into uncharacteristic silence.

It was only when I became a parent that I started to understand that what I had learned from being a poet could help me be a father. That became even more true when I realized that my child was not neurotypical. To be the parents to our child, Sarah and I remind each other that we have to learn to live in negative capability, and also to be not just content, but grateful, to live in half knowledge and contradiction.

*

The last drink I had was on the evening of October 30, 2018. It was at the end of a long, boozy day that had started in the afternoon, at the Hawk 'n' Dove, a bar on Capitol Hill in Washington, D.C. My friend Chicu and I drank and talked and gossiped. I got more and more buzzed. We were participating in a panel at the Library of Congress. Then dinner, where there were more drinks, and at the end of the night, one final, funereal glass of wine. I woke up the next morning, early, and couldn't remember a thing that I or anyone else had said at the panel, or really for the whole day and night. I flew back home so I could go trick-or-treating with my family, feeling horror and shame. Nothing had happened that night, but I knew with absolute certainty it was just a matter of time until I made some truly irreparable mistake.

I don't know what it's like for other people, but for me, alcohol provides absolute certainty. No matter how else I am feeling, I know once I start to drink that I will end up feeling a certain way. My fear, anxiety, self-loathing, shame, disappointment will become muted, then disappear. I will experience an absolutely predictable relief. Whatever happens, or however I feel the next day, the lure of that certainty is so powerful that even describing it now makes me long for it.

At the end of section 6 of "Song of Myself," Whitman writes, "to die is different from what any one supposed, and luckier." John Berryman, in the middle of his Dream Songs, writes, "I had a most marvelous   piece of luck. I died." I love the space between "marvelous" and "luck." I always think of it as indicating the precise instant when the speaker realizes he is, in fact, dead. To die out of the dream of one life and into another is the most terrible, marvelous piece of luck. To live in such uncertainty—which is, as we all eventually find out, where we all are always living—is lonely and requires the ability to not reach for fact, or reason, or solutions, while also constantly reaching for all those things. I am lucky to be a poet, for at least I have learned in writing what I am still trying to learn in life.

*

I take him to speech therapy. Patiently, the therapist asks him to ask *who, what, where. Why* is for later. The questions she is asking are difficult for him. When we first began to bring him, when he was two, we had to teach him to say *mom* and *dad*, to say *yes* and *no*, to point at things, to wave.

I have seen this before, progress incremental, then sudden, then a skill taken for granted and on to the next. He moves too fast, and wants to repeat sentences, paragraphs, whole stories that he remembers unerringly. The sound of them, the material of the language in his mouth and ears and mind, gives him pure pleasure.

We come home through the increasingly smoky air. I don't need to check the news to know it's getting worse. People impatiently explain why it's actually good to separate kids from their parents at the border. I sit down at my desk and write nothing. Just this: At times like this, it feels embarrassing to be a poet. And even more embarrassing to write about it. All this talking to the mirror, pretending it is talking back. The assertion that poetry could do anything that really matters, or stop anything from happening, feels ever more strenuous. I mean, if something is really and truly vital, do you have to make an argument for it? We'd trade all the poetry in the world right now for a good rainstorm, a breath of wind.

When my son began to learn to speak, it became clear that along with a language delay, he was having difficulty distinguishing among pronouns. His facility has grown greatly over the years, with hard work and persistence, but he still often confuses *you* and *I*. "Daddy, you want to go to the park." *You* meaning *I*, and also meaning *I want you to want what I want, so it will happen.*

It's how we speak to him all the time, so he repeats it back to us, which actually makes complete sense. He uses language in the way he remembers it working, like a spell. Sarah and I have learned to rearrange our sentences to avoid saying *you*. Instead of "Do you want to go to the park?," we say, "Let's go to the park!" or "How about we go to the park?" A constant linguistic vigilance that becomes automatic.

How to remind him, without saying some words that he can just automatically repeat and not think through for himself? One of our therapists taught us something simple and effective. *I = eye.* I point to my eye and look at him, without speaking. He pauses and says, "I want to go to the park." I do that so many times a day that it has become completely automatic: listen, point, be silent, wait.

There is something beautiful to me about this dissolution of the pronouns. Maybe his pronoun confusion reflects the shifting borders of desire. When he wants something, he wants us to want it too. His desire for affection and connection is so pervasive that he ignores artificial linguistic borders. It often feels to me like he is living in one great *we*.

*

For a long time, when I wrote *you* or *we* in a poem, I just assumed that my readers were people more or less like me. The distance that obsessed me was between me and potential romantic partners, or friends, or family, or some kind of imagined stranger who carried within their shadowy body some or all of those attributes.

There are experiences humans share, despite their differences: being a child, becoming truly aware of mortality, love lost and gained and lost again, friendship, nature. The qualities of these experiences are deeply shaped by social and economic circumstances, but even within those differences certain experiences resonate among many if not most of us. The provisional assumption that these things might be common is where that *you* or *we* can serve the poem. Yet that assumption can also come at a cost. It can be grasping, and the need not to be alone can obliterate the reality of the other.

"What I assume you shall assume," wrote Whitman. But again, who exactly is that "you"? And who is the "we," named and implied, that suffuses Whitman's work as well? For a long time it was assumed that this "we" and "you" included all of us. In section 6 of "Song of Myself," Whitman writes, of grass:

> I guess it is a uniform hieroglyphic,
> And it means, Sprouting alike in broad zones and narrow zones,
> Growing among black folks as among white,
> Kanuck, Tuckahoe, Congressman, Cuff, I give them the same, I receive them the same.
>
> And now it seems to me the beautiful uncut hair of graves.

Kanuck is a Canadian, and Tuckahoe an Indian tribe. When I look up "Cuff," I see it is something called a "day-name," that is, the name given to any slave, every slave, born on a Friday. I've read this poem hundreds of times without knowing this. A terrible history is contained in that word which so casually appears. How many times has this poem been taught without anyone asking, What is Cuff? Where is the outrage, the despair, the resistance that the use of such a name should produce? When I ask that question, the casualness with which it is spoken, and the casualness in turn with which I have always accepted that this passage is a demonstration of Whitman's democratic and tolerant eye, start to break down.

The "you" that Whitman addresses takes on a more ominous tone. It excludes those who cannot tolerate what he takes for granted, and, in the ease with which I myself feel included, implicates me as well. It feels, well, assumptive, a word I use because instinctively it seems right to me. When I look it up I discover its original meaning is "to seize something for oneself."

So often the pronoun *we* also is used to replace something that would be much more complicated if it were specified. Doesn't "We the people" sound nice? Yes, but who is this "we"? We all know (do we?) it wasn't everyone. Claudia Rankine writes, in *Just Us*: "from this moment forward how easily will the pronoun 'we' slip from my lips?" Not easily at all.

*

Language is only one way of creating a shared reality. And it is only one way to understand the world. But it is also the case that my son, as he speaks more, understands more. The sort of speaking that leads to understanding is painstaking and difficult for him to achieve. Many words come easily to him. They feel good in his mouth, they make him laugh. But the more words he truly internalizes, the more access he has to the shared reality of his parents, his schoolmates, his teachers. I think we might be teaching him not to speak, but to listen, not just to what he hears inside his own head but to more of the world.

Late in his life, the poet Jack Spicer gave a series of lectures in Vancouver in which he asserted some odd and compelling ideas about poetic inspiration. In one of the lectures he posits that poets are receivers, like radios, for alien messages, and the purpose of education, for a poet, is really to give the aliens more tools to work with so that they can say more things.

This is not dissimilar to what Percy Bysshe Shelley wrote in 1821, in "A Defence of Poetry." His essay argues for poetry as a singular form of knowledge, and praises poets for capturing something essential not about themselves, but about their time. According to Shelley, poets are seers: "electric life . . . burns within their words." The final passage is well-known, at least among poets:

> Poets are the hierophants of an unapprehended inspiration; the mirrors of the gigantic shadows which futurity casts upon the present; the words which express what they understand not; the trumpets which sing to battle, and feel not what they inspire; the influence which is moved not, but moves. Poets are the unacknowledged legislators of the world.

That remark about unacknowledged legislators is famous. But it is Shelley's comparison of poets to mirrors in which gigantic shadows of futurity are cast that should haunt us. The art of our time has a constant, helpless prescience. A mirror reflects, but cannot itself see.

Sometimes I feel that for my son, the process of learning language is one of assembling useful phrases that can be employed in various ways. As if he is both the alien trying to communicate and the receiver who is continually gathering more and more tools that will be useful for more and more sophisticated communication. The other day he picked up a roll of blue tape our dog had chewed and, with great seriousness, said, "This seems to have sustained a significant amount of damage." It was funny, and correct. I realized that the phrase was from a video he had watched, in which someone is unpacking a set of trains that they had bought, sight unseen, from the internet.

I was driving home last night, after we left a party. He was happy until we got in the car and he realized that Sarah, who had decided to stay a little longer, wasn't coming with us. He started to sob, and kept saying, "I feel sad that . . ." and then trying to finish the sentence. It was a typical moment: this phrase "I feel sad" is something he was taught, or heard, and he was trying to apply it. He was totally correct about using it, but there was still something a little artificial, as if he had learned a phrase in a foreign language and it was still on the surface, correct but not deep. It was so painful, and wonderful, to watch him try to use language in a way that comes so easily to others. And the most wonderful thing was, he didn't have to use language at all. He could have dissolved into wordless sorrow. But he chose to try, to try to speak, because he knows this is what will get him what he needs, and also because he knows it is how you can make a connection.

And I had this thought, in these words, with their odd, inverted, Biblical syntax, as if they too came to me from somewhere else: Have I not been given a surfeit of feeling? Doesn't my cup overflow with it? What a lucky thing, for me and for him, to have so much joy and pain, to have a life so full of pain and joy.

*

In my observation, language operates for my son more like a dynamic system. The more he understands about the world, the more he looks for words to help him explain, connect, get what he wants. And the more language he uses, the more he understands about the world.

It turns out this is so for nonspeaking autistics as well. I wish everyone would watch "The End of Intellectual Disability? Lessons from Nonspeaking Autism," a video essay made by Dan Bergmann, a nonspeaking autistic who uses alternative modes of communication. In it, he explains and demonstrates that what looks like either a cognitive disability (autistic people cannot understand, because their brains are not properly formed) or a question of motivation (what motivates the autistic person is not what motivates the rest of us, so we need to cajole or lure or punish the autistic person into doing something) is really a question of the body's ability to use language. Under the right circumstances, and with the right support, everyone can communicate. We have to look past our assumptions based on behaviors, which are often an expression of frustration, or a reaction to the environment (intense distraction, or being overwhelmed).

In the video we hear a friendly automated voice translate Bergmann's typed words: "It takes me forever to make my body do anything. I can't even look into the camera and smile. But it turns out that with enough coaching and assistance, nonspeakers like me can be taught to type. And with the ability to make language comes the ability to think abstractly and systematically. And with the ability to think comes the ability to participate in the world. Especially if the world will be a little patient."

I have seen all these things with my son. He works so hard to do so many things that come easily to others, so much harder than anyone I know does at anything. He does it with help, in connection with others. Bergmann describes how he first learned to use language, with assistance in choosing the letters he needed to spell out what he wanted to say. "It's shared attention that pierces the loneliness of autism. The trick is to spell something that is really worth spelling. Then the spelling can be the highlight of both people's day. The spellers I know all enjoy using unusual words that surprise their interlocutors."

Surprise, creativity, connection through communication. This is exactly, of course, what I strive for in making poems. "Attention," wrote Simone Weil, "is the purest form of generosity." Shared attention is the purest form of connection, and shared perseverance through difficulty is what "pierces the loneliness." When my son is making meaning word by word, it's sublime. He looks at me, and I wait as he searches. Sometimes if he needs help I give him a choice of two things I think he might mean, and he either picks one or continues searching. Everything means something and is there for a reason. Around him, no one ever takes a single word for anything less than the treasure it is.

It took me a long time to understand any of this. Language came so easily to me. And when it didn't, in learning Russian, I gave up too easily and could not retain it. My son never forgets anything. So often, he associates whatever he has learned with the person he learned it with. The connection is indistinguishable from the new skill. In his video, Bergmann says, "We can build robots to help us get dressed and maybe even help us write. But we need to do it without eliminating the increased human contact that is the true glory of my life since I learned to spell."

I understand his words, and the experience of my son, by thinking of the difficulty I have in making poems, and of the singular concentration and focus that reading them brings me.

*

Last night he had croup, that barking, infamous cough parents dread. It's an inflammation of the upper respiratory system that sounds of mortal peril. It is usually not dire, but it makes breathing difficult, and is legendarily terrifying for good reasons. We were up most of the night, sitting with him in front of the refrigerator and in the bathroom in the steam. The usual treatment for croup is to immediately bring the child outside, to get moisture that way, from the night air. But that's not possible right now.

Lying in bed at 3 a.m., listening to him cough. He has a high fever and it's the time of night when there are no defenses. All the worries come flooding in. Will he be able to tell us what hurts? A global temperature rise of eight degrees? Ten? Would we all move inland? How many tens of millions of people? At the beginning of the last century, no one could have imagined what awaited them. What awaits us?

Again, I do the math. If I can just live another thirty-five years . . . he'll be nearing forty. Every parent I know is afraid now. Surely parents always have been. But now we are all worried about what sort of world our kids will be living not in, but literally on. Will he understand that world well enough to live on his own, support himself, have a family, friends? Our friends, though they are worried, are mostly not asking themselves those particular questions now, though they will have other difficult questions later.

These questions are unhelpful at this time of night. I think about writing them down. It usually helps, maybe in a false way. It feels good to organize things a little in my mind and then put them down, tinker (I am tinkering right now) to get them right. But to write something down doesn't change anything. Maybe it even makes things worse, by letting us think we have solved something.

Here in the middle of complicated night I wonder, Is there something I could write that would truly help? Not merely to console myself. Or console others, which is probably the last thing anyone needs. Maybe the most important thing is to discover a consolation that does not lead to passivity. I want to be as simple and clear as possible, to reach out to you, without making things simpler and clearer than they actually are, which would be a deep betrayal.

*

Restless, exhausted, unable to sleep, I read yet another article about Rupi Kaur, the most famous living poet in the world, part of a group known as Instagram poets. She puts her poems on social media and millions of people like them, and buy her books. Kaur is a figure of great controversy in the "poetry world," by whom she is usually discussed with condescension at best. Yet her poems resonate with so many people.

I often give a certain untitled poem by Kaur to my students, curious how they will react. In the poem she describes how an unspecified "they" buried her alive, and then she dug her way out of the ground. In response the earth itself "rose in fear and / the dirt began to levitate." Often her poems are accompanied by her drawings. This one has a human figure, arms upraised, rising from what looks like a grave.

When I show this poem to my students, most like it. They say they find it easy to relate to, by which I think they mean that the ideas they pick up from it feel familiar to their own lives. The poem ends with the lines, "my whole life has been an uprising / one burial after another." This analogy of life as a series of burials and uprisings feels to them real, and accurate. It's a manageable and graspable act of the imagination. Some ask me, Why does she use a lowercase "i" to refer to herself in the poem? Why break the sixth line after "and"? I tell them I don't know, and ask them what they think. We talk about why the earth itself might react "in fear" to her survival.

I always hope they will focus on the last word of the penultimate line, "uprising," for its double meaning, personal and revolutionary. That way, we can talk about how a word can be reactivated by a poem, how the way a poem brings our attention to a word we have said a thousand times can make it seem new again, bring its multiple meanings out to collide productively.

Stylistically, Kaur's poems bypass, by design and without apology, the difficulty of poetry. They go straight to the meaning that we are so often told we must search for. It's like every poem is itself the answer on the test about the poem, what you are supposed to get to at the end of the essay you have to write. This certainly can be a relief, especially after reading many poems that seem to deliberately be hiding a message behind a scrim of fancy language, or (better? worse?) to be hiding nothing at all. The recalcitrant, elusive poem doesn't need to be there, it's just a ghost of difficulty, gratefully banished. As if you imagined the paraphrase of the poem without the poem itself.

Kaur's poems are composed mostly of familiar phrases. She seems to be always looking for commonality of experience. In those phrases are realities her readers know well. In her poetry, familiarity is not there as a shortcut, or to hide something or make it easier to take. It exists so that people can put their specific experiences into the generality of the poem, and feel that the poem relates to them. The poem creates community by being generally applicable.

Most of the students like this, and express relief that there is finally something they can understand. Clear, direct communication. This is what everyone says they want in poetry, isn't it? Isn't that what I want from myself, from my son, from all of us? There are always a few grouchy dissenters, though the things those dissenters say are lacking—where is the exciting language? the elaborate metaphors and imagery? the complexity? the hidden meaning?—are actually not what I think usually makes poetry great, or at least, they are not necessary.

Often the best poems are so simple they seem effortlessly transparent, but in a way that opens up more questions than the poem answers. I show the students some haiku along with the Kaur poems.

> the autumn full moon:
> all night long
> I paced round the lake

Spreading a straw mat in the field
I sat and gazed
at the plum blossoms

Those are by Bashō, universally acknowledged as Japan's greatest poet. How are they different from and similar to Kaur's poems? The student answers usually point out the loneliness of the haikus. They say that Kaur, unlike Bashō, helps them feel seen, and feel like they can survive, and are not alone.

*

Survival through reassertion of one's identity and power is a constant theme of Kaur's poems. In one short poem, titled, "what's the greatest lesson a woman should learn?" she writes that every woman already has everything she needs "within herself./ It's the world that/ convinced her she did not." I wonder here about the word "world." I suspect she does not mean this literally, like the globe or the earth itself, but something about society. I long for a little more precision, to know more exactly what she means. Though again, perhaps it is precisely this lack of precision that allows readers to insert whatever particular factors or life experiences they have into poem, which makes them feel connected, and seen.

Kaur's use of the word "world" makes me think of Wallace Stevens: "The house was quiet and the world was calm." Both poets are trying to get to something underneath the particulars, some kind of structure of thinking or feeling that we share. In Kaur's line she is explicitly conjuring up that essence behind the particulars. Stevens's line is general too. But it feels self-conscious, more like a wish. The poem begins, "The house was quiet and the world was calm./ The reader became the book; and summer night/ Was like the conscious being of the book. / The house was quiet and the world was calm."

The speaker is certain of many things. He starts with what he knows to be true, observations that are verifiable, and then moves out from there. He goes on to describe how this unspecified reader (himself? the reader?) "leaned above the page," and then the poem corrects itself: "Wanted to lean, wanted much most to be / The scholar to whom his book is true, to whom // The summer night is like a perfection of thought." There is an aspiration to some perfect state. The poem, like so many lyrics, tragically falls short of some place of comfort, while paradoxically providing comfort to the reader by being together with them in that insufficiency.

Stevens's knowing seems to be about something that cannot really be specified. This poem just keeps circling back in on itself, creating a world that I love to be in, but don't think has much to tell us about anything but itself. I suppose if this poem has a message, it is one that anyone who is reading it already knows: reading is awesome in a certain kind of way where all things melt into each other, and there is such a thing as quiet in the world, however temporary.

There is something odd, though, about the beginning of this very peaceful poem: " . . . and the world was calm." This poem is from *Transport to Summer*, which was published in 1947. I don't know exactly when Stevens wrote it, but whenever he did, the world was definitely not calm. Even if it was during the postwar period, the carnage and destruction, tens of millions dead, concentration camps and firestorms and nuclear bombs, had happened so recently, and must still be there, even if unmentioned.

Whenever I read the poem, I recognize this feeling: of course it is not literally true that "the world is calm," it never is. But it is true that it can *feel* calm for a little while. This is a delusion. Maybe a necessary one, in order to allow one to regain a little strength. Or maybe this wish is aspirational. One day the world could be calm, if only we all had the time and space and safety and freedom to read a book on a summer night when there was nothing to worry about.

Which raises several questions in which the poem seems quite uninterested. For whom is the world safe, even occasionally? Who does this reader stand in for, and who is not included? What does that safety for those very few cost the many, figuratively and literally? Can we imagine a world where not just a few but everyone gets to experience the peaceful calm of a quiet house? Why is one person's ordinary evening in New Haven very unlike another's? We know the answers. Money. Race. Class. Privilege. The limitation of this poem is in its assumption that everyone reading it has access to this peace. I don't feel Kaur would ever make that assumption.

I have always believed a great poem cannot be paraphrased. You can be in conversation with it, or attempt to describe what you see in it. But it cannot be reduced. It has no single theme or answer that can be tested. The better the poem, the more impossible it is to sum up its meaning. "Extreme clarity is a mystery," writes Mahmoud Darwish. But sometimes, in situations of great urgency, we require a different sort of clarity, one that is less mysterious. A call to action. I don't think it is easy to achieve that sort of clarity in a poem without it turning into a sermon. But I also don't think it is easy to achieve mysterious clarity in a poem that does not slide into irrelevance or self-absorption.

*

Like Kaur, I am deeply attracted to simplicity. Yet I also instinctively shy away from language that feels too public or euphemistic. Probably I am afraid that I will get sucked up into the great machine of collective thought, and lose my ability to resist . . . something, I'm not even sure what. Maybe it's just my Gen X programming.

Despite all this, despite my best efforts, lately I find whole phrases coming out of my mouth that I realize, somewhere along the way, were focus-group-tested algorithms. This terrifies me. Whether or not these ideas are somewhat or mostly accurate is irrelevant. There is a way that ideas of all sorts worm their way into our minds. Surely this is because I am so constantly consuming so much news. But this happens regardless of whether we are regular users of social media, or even a computer. It's no wonder that the virus is the central metaphor of our time.

The originality and singularity of our own experiences is constantly belied. Maybe the fact that there is nothing original about those experiences, is not a problem, but a virtue. What do I really, truly know? I know simple things: I love my son, his little bear pajamas, my wife, the grass, the poems I read . . . actually, a lot of things that are not mere information. "All the world is all of us," says one of his favorite books. Maybe everything belongs to everyone, and is waiting to be returned.

POEM FOR RUPI KAUR

Lying in bed at 3am
listening to him cough
in his bear pajamas
is not fun
there is no joy
right now
or ever now
that I know
my heart lives
outside my body
in him and the grass

and my wife
because you wrote
defeated eyes
I know you understand
how I feel
when I say
the high fever of night
there are no defenses
again I do the math
will I live long enough
to see him thrive
in what sort of world
we are living
not in but on
you know what I mean
one of the continents
is on fire
you are not
wrong to think
in poems
we can solve
something complicated
a lot of things
are not information
here in the middle
of complicated night
it has become clear
we cannot trust
the central metaphor
which is we are children
though it is true
we are not
safe anywhere
I love my son
his little bear pajamas
my wife the grass
the ends of poems

Tunnel Park

I get him ready for school and then drop him off and then go to
school myself. Today, one student sits in my office and asks, Is
my poem good? It's the question every poet so desperately wants
answered, and the longer a poet writes, the more they know it is
the wrong question. What do you mean "good"? I say, stalling. By
whose standards? Those of an imagined editor, publisher? An ideal
reader, who needs nothing and cannot ever be pleased? Some end-
lessly receding figure of a mother or father? Who do you imagine
will be listening, and how does that shape what you make?

The student and I sit in silence. The air outside is the smokiest it
has been. I don't know how to say, in a way that does not hide what
I too am always asking myself about the poem I am trying to write
and have put away but still think about: Maybe the question is not
is the poem good, but how can it become at last strange enough to
cross over?

Aristotle wrote that poets are poets because they make metaphor.
They are fitters. They put together things we think are strangers
to each other. This makes them a danger to all authorities. Their
profanity is holy, and in every word they write, they assert the pos-
sibility that we can cross between worlds to make new meaning.

In their arrogant hope, they connect things that do not belong
together. They intuit relationships between things that are ordi-

narily hidden. They love to reconcile differences in a magical alchemy that preserves the integrity of the elements. See this metaphor, this magic trick, how two unlike things stay unalike and come together to form meaning. They also, despite everything, leap across the voice to connect their consciousness to another's. Despite everything, they believe in the possibility of listening.

Poetry is flashes of insight, moments of partiality (what Keats called "fine isolated verisimilitudes") intermixed with odd statements that seem to encompass the truth, deep emotions and symbols that appear and cannot be resisted. García Lorca's eyes of cold silver. Elizabeth Bishop's Marvel stove. James Tate's burning snowflake. Kim Hyesoon's temple made of thread, blowing around in the wind.

Poetry is a joke. An accordion solemnly playing a clam. It seems to look down on us looking down on it, sorrowfully bemused.

Supposedly the air should become "good" again later today, then get worse, then finally clear up next week, rain and air blowing the smoke into the ocean. I feel like if I concentrate hard enough, the trapped air will start to move away, over the water, through the gate over the sea, where it can't hurt anyone.

*

And now I am informed the air is getting a little better. I just got a text from the powers telling me it is currently orange, an improvement over the hazardous purple and problematic red. This orange feels *aspirational*, a word that seems suddenly to be doing a lot of work, like lungs.

I keep coming back to the poem I'm supposed to be writing for this book, and now I don't feel anything. My fear that all this focus on writing it, this writing about writing, will kill any intuition, seems to be coming true. Sometimes the poems come so easily, it is a mystery, as if they were waiting to be found, and all that is necessary is to write down the words, almost like tracing something that was invisibly on the page. At other times, no amount of pushing, experimenting, launching oneself in an instinctive direction, picking out words from the dictionary, reading other people's poems, cutting up the lines and rearranging them . . . nothing works. Does the traffic really sound like a train under the sea? Like a black tunnel?

When it is hard to write, everything I type just feels dead. The most obvious, immediate associations and conclusions cannot follow what precedes them; that would make the poem dead on arrival. On the other hand, a willed weirdness, an arbitrary surrealist or whimsical or just jokey type of thinking feels too light on the page, unworthy of a reader's attention. "Poetry is the way we help give name to the nameless so it can be thought," writes Audre Lorde, and if I am not giving name to the nameless, but merely replicating emptiness, I feel with myself a horrible echo.

*

Tonight at last it rained, and the air cleared. The fire is mostly put out up north. A channel to the ocean has opened and the smoke is flowing out through the narrow Golden Gate. It is not hard for me to visualize this climactic event. I can feel it, a withdrawal, the creation of a necessary emptiness, room to start living again.

*

Listening to Haydn this morning is comforting, and also makes me feel like a fraud. I enjoy it and also feel like I am enjoying my enjoying being someone who listens to classical music. Is this how people feel reading poetry? Who cursed poetry with importance? It's the most unimportant thing I can imagine. It barely exists. It's like a candle in the wind, never knowing who to cling to, when the rain set in. "Candle in the Wind" is, scientifically speaking, the worst song ever written. According to the internet it is a threnody, a "wailing ode."

Other examples of threnody include: "Ohio" by Crosby, Stills, Nash and Young, "Since I Lost You" by Genesis, and "Threnody to Earth" by Dream Koala. Apparently this is a cursed genre. I admit I am tempted to listen to Dream Koala, but both the band name and the song title are so great I am sure listening will be a disappointment. Haydn's late sonatas occasionally get slow and seem like threnodies to something unnamed.

The truth is, I can't write the poem. I have nothing to say, or maybe too much. Sometimes you have to put it in a drawer, and try to forget about it. Once you finally do, it will come to mind again when you have finally forgotten enough to allow the solution to arrive, unbidden.

I also have nothing more to say about poetry. Except that at every moment, when I am in a meeting about my son, when I am at the gym, or answering emails while refusing to listen to Dream Koala, instead to Glenn Gould playing Haydn's late sonatas or to my friend Missy's extraordinary, singular band Victoire, or walking past the marquee in Oakland that says Kurt Vile, my heart filling with happy regret that instead of going to see that show I am going to dinner with my wife and some old friends who are moving to Australia with their two resentful teenage sons, or organizing books on my shelf instead of reading them, or looking futilely for my lost backpack, or eating a green apple I dropped in the road and then washed and was so pleased to find was mostly not bruised, or feeling the slight despair of the evening coming on and knowing I have to go out to loyally see one of my former students read poetry in San Francisco, where I will listen and not drink because I no longer drink alcohol, and try not to buy books because my house is filled with unread volumes that already hold the key to everything, or when I am coming home and hoping that she is still awake, I am always remembering what it feels like to be in that blessed state of putting the words together, without any ideas, just moving words and phrases around almost without thought and with total freedom to at last see those connections that were waiting there so patiently until I could stop trying to force things to be what they were not, moving them with no thought at all, mostly just a sense of what should go with what in order to make the meaning I can almost grasp, and then can feel like a spell as it starts to come together, a physical sensation like making something out of air in the air with my hands, but even after I take my hands away it somehow remains.

*

The harmonium is a foot-powered organ, and sounds inherently anachronistic. I imagine something smallish, wooden, a keyboard held in an ornately carved, delicately painted cabinet. I know my neighbor has one, because once, after I heard some music coming from her window (our houses are unusually close), we discussed it. She told me she used to play for her church, but now she just plays it at home, a statement that seemed to hold an entire unwritten novel behind it.

This morning, she is playing again. Spooky compositions I don't recognize—perhaps they are improvisations—leak from her window into ours. To listen feels like a private concert, and a private joke, since the time and day she is playing is also the name of the most famous poem in Wallace Stevens's first book, *Harmonium*. "Sunday Morning" begins in the mind of a woman who doesn't go to church, and instead stays home to have her private reveries. I feel this moment was constructed exactly for the only person around who would appreciate it.

As the creaky music streams in the window, my past enters too. Endless days living in a house in suburbs not unlike this one. Quiet holidays, waiting for something that never arrived. Snow, going out with my brother to shovel it and the neighbor's walk (we took the dollar bills, three of them, with our mittens). Long summers, hopping the low fence to the basketball hoop next door. Going to school with a vague sense of excitement, never fulfilled. I knew I wanted to do something besides read and wait and wonder about the other kids, what they were happily discussing. All the names coming back to me now. Giant clouds moved across the sky, above the American elms and slow-growing American beeches, both of which can easily grow to over one hundred feet tall.

Of course, there are trees famous for being even huger here. Last week, I was standing outside with someone in our yard, both of us wearing masks. We were discussing what plants could be drought resistant and maybe even beneficial. He pointed out casually that about ten feet away from us was a sequoia in our neighbor's backyard.

I had been out there hundreds of times and never noticed it. Later, I went out again and got right up to the fence, so I was under the canopy. Standing under it I looked up through the smoky air along its dry rivulets of darker and lighter brown, up into the branches and the dark green leaves. I could smell something powerful that transcended the smoke.

Suddenly the music stops. Soon, my son will wake up, and immediately start building some complex structure. Over the course of the day, our house gets gradually filled with drawings he tapes to the wall, his books everywhere, and tracks, gracefully curved up and over the furniture and onto perilously elevated bridges braced with any available material (books, chairs, even piled-up laundry, possibly clean) then back down, running around and over and through smartly designed buildings made of a mixture of Legos, wooden blocks, magnetic tiles, and anything else available. At the end of each day we pack it all up, and each morning he starts again. Along the way, there will be many demands to help him build, or to sit and draw cars, trains, rocket ships, snowmen, tunnels, bridges, houses, cities. Recently he figured out how to draw in perspective, how I have no idea, since I am not capable of teaching him. And all the while, the house will be filled with singing. He has perfect pitch and remembers any melody he hears, even once, forever. Help, he sings, and tower to the skies.

*

One of my son's great talents is his memory. His recall is clean and instantaneous. It's why in a poem I call him "remembrancer," stealing an archaic word from Whitman's "Song of Myself." Yet that memory can at times also interfere with his ability to be present. When he sees someone he knows, he sings the song they first sang together. This is beautiful and singular, but it also means his mind is doing one thing, and not something else that would put him closer to the actual moment he is in. He is aware of the present moment, but his attention is divided. There is only so much a mind, even a very clever one, can do.

And all the time he hears the voices he has heard, in songs and in books, from his parents and teachers and friends. They come to him so easily, maybe too easily.

He likes to say or hear one word and then rhyme it, sonically, with another word, and then use that word to remind him of a book or song or event. *Cantaloupe* to *candle* to thinking about the candles we light on Shabbat, which is his favorite, he knows all the blessings by heart and loves to look at the candles and sing the songs . . . we light the candles and gather the light three times, then cover our eyes with our gathering hands to keep the light for a little while inside us. He has a swimming teacher named Kendall, whom he calls Teacher Candle.

When his speech therapist said that his mind is powerfully drawn to associative thinking, I literally startled. Along with metaphor, associative thinking and conceptual rhyme are basic mechanisms of poetry, forms of association. To "rhyme" one concept with another, not by sound, but by finding hidden, intuitive commonalities, is to make the connection that animates poetry. Basically, this is another way of describing the mechanism of a metaphor, which, as Aristotle so accurately defined it, is the connection of one thing or concept to another that is surprising (alien) but, once it is made, reveals a heretofore unseen resemblance. For better and worse, my son is susceptible to conceptual rhyme in his thinking, drawn to make connections that interest him regardless of their usefulness or relevance to what is going on around him.

Words send him off into associations. You can say "actor" and he will think and say "tractor," then recite the book about tractors. He thinks in rhyme, as I also say in the poem. It's hard for him to stay present, maybe because he does not want to, or because it is confusing for him, and safer and clearer to go by association into the world of memory. I don't know. It's extremely interesting and entertaining and awesome to see this, and also terrifying, so clearly to see him marked by difference in this world designed for so-called normal thinkers. Is there a way for him to use his great memory as a strength, and also be present? To turn more of his mind and intelligence in the direction of what is happening now, the subtleties of social interaction, people's faces and voices, while never losing his singularity? I believe so.

*

I drive to school and sit in an empty classroom. Outside, it is raining, and I am thinking about teaching. This fall I had my first sabbatical ever, and devoted it to this one poem I am trying to write, and to writing about writing it, here. Just a little over a month and it will be the new year, and I will need to remember how to teach.

In my syllabus I quote the first stanza of one of my favorite poems, by Antonio Machado:

> Last night as I was sleeping,
> I dreamt — marvelous error! —
> that a spring was breaking
> out in my heart.
> I said: Along which secret aqueduct,
> Oh water, are you coming to me,
> water of a new life
> that I have never drunk?

It is a perfect poem about nothing and everything. It sings, asks questions, repeats. Marvelous error, aka life, are you bringing to me some good new water?

I have made so many errors, so few of them marvelous. I say to the students: If you would like, I can show you places in your poems (not in your lives) where you might have missed that you were making a marvelous error, one that only your weird imagination and no other was capable of making. Here, look, without knowing it you corrected yourself back into what is normal, acceptable, agreed-upon, banal.

I keep on forgetting, then learning again, that in poems, I can start anywhere, no matter how terrible, and revise and rethink and change and add. The necessary poem will eventually emerge. As long as I get something down. Somehow, I figured out in writing what I still cannot seem to learn in life. I can't seem to remember that whatever is going on, it is possible to change it. To revise it.

I sit in the empty classroom and think about the poem I am supposed to be working on. I hope, while it sleeps in a drawer, that I can forget it, until I learn whatever will help me finish it. I am thinking too about what my students need to forget. They have absorbed so much, without knowing it, about what makes a poem literary and good. I was the same way. It took me a long time to forget, to stop writing "poetry" so I could begin to write it.

My students carry ideas about poetry inside them, ones that they heard from the outside and were not asked for. They fall back on those as soon as their own writing gets truly dangerous and real. They also, each in a singular configuration, because of their backgrounds and personal history, carry ideas about themselves: fears of appearing a certain way, of failing or being laughed at or seen as insufficient, not belonging, not enough. It is my job to point out to them, gently, where they might be avoiding the truth of the poem, their own truths, in order to protect themselves.

I have also learned that so many of them have experienced past or traumas (or are experiencing them now) that they are only beginning to come to terms with, in their poems as in their lives. It can be too difficult for them to talk directly about these things, too early. So they hide where it is safe, temporarily, in ambiguous language or symbols only they can understand. In their struggles, they seem stronger than I will ever be.

Whenever I start writing again after a pause, sometimes even a short one, like them I too feel overwhelmed and blocked by all my ideas about what I "should" do, what I "want" the poems to be. I don't even know I have them. But they interfere and make the poems false, and it takes some time and courage and honesty to once again identify the problem, and get past it, to do what is necessary. What is necessary is not something I can perceive or think my way into, I have to err into it.

*

I was born into an upper middle class household, the child of children of immigrants. Even though my parents were interested in art and culture, and in certain ways unconventional for their time, basically they were establishment people. My father was the son of a dressmaker who was born in the old country, came to Brooklyn and eventually moved to Dallas and started his own factory. My grandfather had ups and downs in business. So my father's childhood years were intermittently marked by financial hardship and instability. He turned out to be a brilliant lawyer, with a secret, dreamy side. He would come home from work and sit in the dark and play Bob Dylan and Elizabeth Cotton songs to himself on his old guitar from law school. What was he thinking? He was far from a rebel. He ultimately believed in order. We were surrounded by order. We lived in a government town. The structures kept us safe, even as they revealed and continually reinvested themselves as being monstrous, especially in the terrible 1980s, with Reagan's grinning skull face and the obvious racial divisions of Washington, D.C., the gleeful violence of the government, its hypocrisy, and our own.

In my high school years in suburban Maryland, I started to perceive exciting and exceptional little futile flares of resistance around me, in the punk rock community in D.C. I was too scared to fully join in. I just stood on the outside of the circle and watched with admiration and awe as these kids got together in communities and fought back, with music and demonstrations and just their presence. They looked and acted different. Some of them had immense, spiked hair, tattoos, metal in their faces. They moved among the conformist, bureaucratic capital city like dark ghosts of reminder and reproach. They would be yelled at, spit on, bullied, beaten up on the street. It took great courage to reject the conventional life that was offered, however empty its consolations might have been, and try to make something new. I have always felt like there was an alternate life there, a possibility that I turned away from, out of fear, without even knowing I was turning away.

I was born bright and quick. Made dark by experience, or experience echoed with the darkness I brought into the world. That quickness, especially in reading and writing and speaking, was valorized and rewarded. This meant I so often went too fast, and did not read or think or speak as carefully and deeply as I could have. I didn't, and so often still do not, perceive what is around me. Paradoxically, along with quickness, certainty was valued too. The fastest one to the right answer wins. Sarah too was born to succeed in this world. We both went to the best schools, got the correct grades, and were always the praised ones. However miserable we might have been, we were always the oldest children who knew all the answers. Our story was the story of success, of an inexorable march toward achievement, normality, prosperity.

My judgment of others and myself can cause me to be angry, and quick to criticize. It can cause me to be impatient with any failing, in myself or others. And it has, to my deep shame, caused me at times to turn away from what is different. There was something inside myself I did not want to listen to. I started to hear it only when, from the moment he was born, I fell in love with my son, and continued to love him more and more as he became who he is, despite my narrow desires and expectations.

I didn't realize how deeply buried in me this story was, until I was forced to see that holding onto it would ruin my life. This is not an exaggeration—holding on to that story truly can cause me pain and grief from moment to moment. I know this because, over the past years, this holding so often has. The days have been excruciating. I have felt like I am in the wrong story, and that all the meaning I was without knowing depending on had suddenly dissolved. I have been sorely tempted to hide our family away from the world, or to hide myself and do other things that will obliterate my consciousness, if only for a few hours.

At other times I feel completely calm, as if life is much bigger and more full of different ways to be than I had thought. This realization is not an intellectual one, not an idea: I know that there are lots of different ways to live and to be happy. It is a spiritual or even bodily realization. I feel, yes, fear and anxiety for my own son's future, but also something else. What would happen if I imagined everything I think is different, "bad," a mistake, all of it is the essential prerequisite for something truly interesting and different? Maybe it is not too late to author my own interesting family structure, relationship to my child, to my wife, to myself? Maybe that is really what I have been waiting not to turn away from, to listen to.

The story I thought was in – which, to be honest, was bringing me very little happiness, and a lot of shame over the inequities upon which it depends – changed, and keeps changing. I've been given this great, unexpected, difficult gift. My challenge is to take everything I have learned, and live up to my story, and my love for my son. Whenever I do, I feel an unfamiliar peace. I still have so much work to do, so much to forget.

*

I have learned how much easier it is to go to work than to write, how much easier to sink into the irritating obligations imposed from elsewhere, to compose one more email, to complain about having no time. There will always be more work than time, and if one is in the mood to agree to take on even more work, it will surely arrive. Agree to do more than the absolute minimum to keep your job and you are doomed. Agree, agree, and suddenly years have passed.

Today I had a meeting with one of the many well-meaning administrators, and in the course of it started agreeing to anything she said. I was being a very good listener, I had fastened on my listening face. I was agreeing that internships are important, that service is important, that importance is important. She could have suggested that I go upstairs and write a short to medium-length proposal to outlaw poetry and I would have gladly listened actively and actively agreed that this proposal was quite important. I would have met her where she was. I would have interrupted her to demonstrate how well I had been listening, to preemptively agree.

No amount of seeds chattering could stop me from agreeing. We talked about service. The redwoods sighed. She is a well-meaning administrator. Her leg stiffens up if she sits for too long. This reminds me of the first time that I went to meet with our department chair, who I only found out much later had desperately wanted to give someone else, really anyone else, the job I had just accepted. I have many times since wished that she had gotten her way. After the meeting where it became immediately clear I now had many obligations that had nothing to do with teaching, I got up to walk down the hall and experienced such an incredible pain in my otherwise completely structurally sound left knee that I could actually barely walk. I leaned against the wall, panting. It was, of course, funny, and there was no one to share the joke with, except the Xerox machine. There could have been no clearer signal. My body knew that I was doing something I did not want to do.

I ignored my body unlike the Californian I am not, and now my body and I are coming to a different sort of agreement. We have agreed not to pour alcohol into it and also to exercise and not to eat more than is necessary. When I am in the shower and for a few moments an interstice of bright afternoon light shines in, I remember my life is a series of marvelous errors, nothing but errors, and that also *error* is the wrong word. It almost makes me feel like I am bathing outdoors, and I become significantly more happy than I have been for the entire day, really happy for the first time in days. Then it is over. My day and I are coming to some kind of agreement. It says what it needs, and I give it. Here I go off into the rain.

*

This rainy Sunday morning I finally finished *The Banished Immortal*, the blue book about Li Bai (whom some call Li Po) by Ha Jin. A finely painted portrait on the cover, his face looking upward, a red sash, white robes with green piping and some blue around the waist and shoulders, one red shoe peeking out. Even he stood in front of Yellow Crane Tower and didn't want to go in and read someone else's poem written on the wall, knowing it would be better than anything he could write, at least at that moment.

Most of his life he was miserably convinced he was a failure because he wasn't an advisor to the emperor, and he even got himself thrown in jail late in life for supporting a rebellion. But even then, all over the empire, people were singing his words, and to this day, a thousand years later, everyone knows his poems and his name.

One of my favorite stories from the book tells how he fell in love with a neighboring widow, so he wrote her a poem, tied it to an arrow, and shot it into her yard. Except that she had moved away. Like many of his peers, he believed that he could discover the secret of immortality by grinding up various toxic substances and making pills that he would then take, to detrimental effect.

There's one fragment of a poem in the introduction that I can't find the rest of anywhere. Ha Jin must have only translated these lines, and I don't know how much of the poem it even is, which makes me frustrated and thrilled:

Night Trip in Gulang

As a young child, I had no idea what the moon was
And I called it a white jade plate.
Then I wondered if it was a mirror at the Jasper Terrace
That flew away and landed on top of green clouds.

Maybe that's the whole poem. I hope so, and not.

Sometimes when my own poems successfully resist me, I like to irresponsibly rewrite translations. I have done this with most of the translations of Li Bai that I own (though not any of the ones by Ha Jin), picking from all the different translations to make my own personal version in English. Here is one of those hybrid stolen versions of a poem Li Bai wrote from the aforementioned Yellow Crane Tower, one of the four great towers of China, which was in Jiangxia, a busy port and center for the arts in Li Bai's time, now known as Wuhan.

Standing on Yellow Crane Tower, Saying Goodbye to Hao-Jan as He Leaves for Yang-Chou

From Yellow Crane Tower I watch my old friend leave the west.
He is going downstream, surrounded by mists and blossoms.

His lone sail glints then vanishes into the emerald air.
Nothing left but the river, flowing off into heaven.

Suddenly I hear thunder, an extremely rare sound here in Northern California. I think of the huge storms that were a regular feature of my youth back in Maryland. I remember I used to feel comforted, inside the house, as the sky grew dark and the huge trees began to shake. Now lightning strikes are to be feared, because they can start a fire so hot it will burn for weeks and destroy anything in its path, even our oldest redwoods.

*

We have a pump in our basement that is supposed to turn on when it detects water flooding in. Maybe it is, like everyone else in this house, exceedingly sensitive. Or perhaps it detects phantom water, or the idea of it. For whatever reason, even though there is no flood, all night it turns on and off with a hum at the exact frequency to trip the switch that jolts me violently out of sleep. The other night Sarah gave me a pair of blue foam earplugs, and maybe it was a placebo effect, but I slept most of the night. But then I lost them. Where could they have gone? Back to the blue mother.

I know we (meaning the land and us) could use the rain. I often feel such painful nostalgia for those years in the past when it rained and it didn't seem to be important, it was just what happened. That mood of quiet boredom and also appreciation of how much more lovely things always look when it is raining, at least from inside the house.

The pump continually startles me awake. There are little breaks and then the rain starts again, in more earnest. And then the pump too. We can all agree theoretically that it's good to have the rain for the reservoirs and rivers and mountains and lakes, but it is more than a bit painful to remember that not too long ago the air was so full of smoke we could not breathe, and most of us were praying for even a few hours of this water. Now it has caused the Russian

River, eighty miles north of us, to rise to forty-five feet, flooding houses, cars completely underwater.

When I imagine a flood I think of pure water, but of course it's full of debris, ugly and brown, and god knows what else is in there. The mind is always willing to purify. Sarah says it's not even going to matter that there has been all this rain, it actually might make things worse, just as it did this fire season, because there will be even more new growth, for the next power line to fall on, or cigarette to be thrown into.

*

Across the street from my office, they are still working on that giant building. I think of the Frank O'Hara poem "Cambridge," which I fell in complete love with, holding that pocket-sized book twenty-five years ago. *Lunch Poems*. The poem begins, "It is still raining" and goes on to talk about how unpleasant it is outside, his hot plate, what he's wearing: "I / put on my warm corduroy pants, a heavy maroon sweater, / and wrap myself in my old maroon bathrobe. Just like Pasternak / in Marburg . . ." The mention of Pasternak leads him to talk in most of the second half of the poem about poetic inspiration, and then end with those amazing last lines: "Across the street, there is a house under construction, / abandoned to the rain. Secretly, I shall go to work on it." I love that "shall." Exactly as formal as it should be in this case, not "will" but "shall," like the quest of a knight.

There is the faint and probably exaggerated implication that the work on the house has not been temporarily but permanently halted, because of the slightly overdramatic word "abandoned," instead of something uninterestingly accurate. It's the very exaggeration of "abandoned," the pathetic fallacy (sense of projection of the emotional state of the poet onto the landscape), a bit knowingly overwrought, ironic and sweet at the same time, that gives that whole moment a texture and subtlety and intensity. I think I learned so much about how to write from poems like this by O'Hara, ones that are a bit more low-key than his most famous ones, but still contain his immense charm.

The unstated comparison is that writing a poem, or being artistically inspired, is like secretly going to work on a house under construction abandoned because of the practical obstacle of rain. Paul Valéry writes, "The best work is that which keeps its secret longest." Brenda Hillman says, "Revise toward strangeness." Bob Hass says, "Put the problem in the poem."

*

In a break in the rain, I took him to his favorite park. It was built in the early part of the twentieth century, when during the Great Depression the government paid people to work on projects that would benefit everyone. It still does. It has a large wooden trolley car that kids climb all over, and a tunnel under the busy street that connects the park to the famous Berkeley Rose Garden, a tourist attraction, as well as a very long cement slide that would be impossible to imagine anyone having the foolish disregard of liability nowadays to even consider constructing. Trains and tunnels are two of his favorite things, so he calls it either "train park" or "tunnel park," depending on his mood.

The park also has various anachronistic paths and stairways that used to lead to pavilions. Kids wander up and down those too. This time I was drawn to the longest stairway in the park. It rises to some unknown destination. He and I started upward, and after a short while, all sounds disappeared. It was just us, walking upward for what seemed like an impossibly long time, until we emerged on some street I had never seen before. A gorgeous old pastel mansion that seemed uninhabited was surrounded by sleeping construction equipment. It felt as if we had penetrated into a realm devoid. No humans. They had all disappeared. We looked at this ghost house for a while, then headed back down, gradually, toward the noise, holding hands, stopping only so he could drink a little from what he calls his "blue water."

Once I was home, this poem came easily. There is time to add it to the book, though it is still not the poem I need, nearly forgotten, sleeping unfinished in the drawer.

TUNNEL PARK

eighty years ago
during those
famous dark times

when the government
paid men to build
bridges and dams

they carved this park
my son loves
out of a hill

the men needed
to keep working
to get paid

so they made
a long dangerous concrete
slide kids scream

down their parents
watching with
their hands

over their mouths
then dug
this unnecessary

cool aperture
full of obscure
shadows through

the hillside
to the garden
of famous roses

I don't care about
and finally some
secret stairs

no matter how many
times we have found
always seem

like they were
forever waiting
only for us

my son and I
went upward
his red shirt

kept disappearing
into the shadows
I became tired

from pointless worry
so we sat on
one stone step

and shared
some blue water
through the leaves

we could see
a giant crumbling
pastel house

it once was grand
its dark windows
still look down

on everything
it was so quiet
I could hear

the message
everyone knows
worse times

are coming
who isn't afraid
only the dead

we went further
the stairs never ended
we had to turn

back to our lives
knowing there is
mystery even

in the new world

(from *Father's Day*)

Hello Everyone, Hello You

When I lived in New York in the early 2000s, one of my favorite places was the Isamu Noguchi Museum in Long Island City. I first heard Noguchi's name in connection with those oddly shaped, bulbous paper lamps that feature in many first apartments. They are made from the soft inner bark of a mulberry tree stretched across a bamboo frame, which gives them their unmistakable organic white color. Noguchi based his construction on a traditional method of making Gifu lamps (after the Japanese town of the same name), molding them into unusual shapes. He called them *akari*, which, according to the museum website, in Japanese means "light as illumination, but also implying the idea of weightlessness."

I did not feel weightless going to the Noguchi museum. Reeling from a humiliating, traumatic breakup, and barely functional from a high dose of antidepressants, I lugged myself through my miserable, uninspired days. I went to his museum in desperate, numbed search of some ideas, something to write about or from, or maybe just some relief.

The museum is a large industrial building, a series of rooms full of Noguchi's sculptures and drawings as well as short films about his life. Polished stones perch all throughout the museum and outside, in the garden. I felt uncharacteristically relaxed there.

Even describing it now I can feel what it was like, the cool darkness permeated with smooth, brightly colored shapes.

I decided to go repeatedly and take notes and write a long poem. I went several times, and took the notes and worked on the poem, which turned out to be terrible. The longer I worked on it, the terribler it got. The problem was that the poem transcribed what I saw in a way that wanted to be symbolic or resonant, but was not. One time when I went to the museum, I saw a few women standing together talking about one of the sculptures outside in the garden:

Four middle-aged women
ghosts draped in furs
walk among the gardens.

They are standing before the fountain
that collects in the east,
but here disperses.

They are discussing which contemptible akari
(sculpture of light)
would look best on the piano.

This is not only boring, but mean. It's also a complete projection and hypocrisy, because not only did I myself have a knockoff version of one of those *akari* lanterns in my very own room, but I adore buying postcards and other mementos in museum gift shops. Sometimes it's hard for me to resist doing so before I see the actual show.

In other places, the poem is just pointlessly weird. I'm trying to find the right tone, but I oscillate between forced lyricism, a willed profundity that often veers into what now seems like a parody of fake haiku "wisdom," and a pretend kind of understatement, all often in the space of a few lines. The poem is practically a catalog of poetic failure, and painful to reread:

Looking for Noguchi

1.

I went with my brothers to look for Noguchi.

It had rained many years
since shoulder to shoulder
in California with axes composed
of music resistance and concern.

And I had learned so much about other things.

...

4.

Weeping cherry, smiling katsuro.
It's so hard to find
a way into the mind.

...

7.

Noguchi says he's in the obsidian.
But that looks like me
in the obsidian.

8.

Look how
cast by shadows
of sculptures

the floor is a sculpture

of monkeys
by monkeys

of overwrought solitude
bowed
in the chapel

   I honestly don't even know what I'm saying at the end of that section. There might have been a sculpture of monkeys, but it sure wasn't made by them, and it is hard to imagine monkeys bowing to anything, in a chapel or elsewhere. Besides just being ridiculous, the main problem here, as with so many poems, is that the consciousness in relation to the content is not genuine. It's more or less all stance, and lying. No amount of making things more "creative" or "imagistic" would help, and in fact, the almost manic effort to be poetic is precisely the problem. I was not ready to write this poem, because I did not yet understand what drew me to that museum, to Noguchi, to his art, which I loved but had nothing to say about yet.

*

A poem is not mere reportage. It is an enactment of a relationship between consciousness and the world. That stance, that relationship, is something that happens to the reader, in real time, when reading the poem. For the poet, it can take a long time to uncover, before it can be reproduced. It has to be discovered anew in each poem. It is also, mysteriously, bound up in form and sound: the way the poem appears on the page, moves down the page, and sounds in the mind and bones of the person reading it . . . these musical factors are inextricable from the poem's personality. In a way, a poem is almost like a personality. W. H. Auden: "A poem might be called a pseudo-person."

Wallace Stevens described the difference between mere reality ("things as they are") and the reality in a poem. Things must be, as he writes, changed upon the blue guitar. Or, as Dickinson writes, tell all the truth but tell it slant, not in order to be deliberately obscure or elusive, but because oftentimes seeing things at a different angle—a slant—allows you to perceive what you could not before. Like an eclipse.

*

I was so depressed and bored with my own depression, and thought to myself, dimly, The only way I am going to get out of this is to feel again what it is like to write poems. That was the only thing I could remember that brought me joy. So I kept returning to the museum, scribbling, taking notes, going back to my dark apartment and trying to assemble them. I still felt nothing.

Halfway through the original draft of the bad poem I was failing to compose as I returned again and again to the Noguchi museum, I wrote: "The garden looks out over the river / facing west / and in another direction / on my apartment / looking out on Brooklyn / Brooklyn / Brooklyn's a row / of dented Sundays."

Here is the glimmer of a strange and, therefore, authentic feeling. One good moment amid all the ridiculousness. I threw away much of it, rebuilding around rare moments of weird clarity to make a new poem called "Brooklyn with a New Beginning," which eventually appeared in my second book. The new poem was not about the Noguchi museum at all. Here is part of it:

> Recently someone's dying screenwriter brother
> has rented me a late morning window full
> of late morning ghosts
>
> who watch me watching
> an elm.
> In early autumn appearance it runs
>
> an already grey wrinkled hand
> over the face
> of a brownstone glittering in September,
>
> alone among the furniture I walk
> thinking this apartment in Brooklyn
> looks out on Brooklyn
>
> Brooklyn
> Brooklyn's a row
> Brooklyn's a row of dented Sundays,
>
> full of terrible laughter
> from the apartment below ...

For too long I was too attached to the initial thought, of writing about Noguchi. This was keeping me from finding the poem I needed to write. That confusion about what the poem is really about was mirrored in the earlier draft by a basic technical problem: sitting in the museum and thinking about sitting both there and in my apartment in Brooklyn is needlessly complicated. It requires a lot of directional language (in my apartment, back here in the museum) that is annoying and boring. It asks the reader to do a lot of pointless separating and categorizing.

Part of learning to write poetry is realizing that you are building a structure that a reader will enter. Or finding the right structure to contain and support the best lines. Like being a dream architect. I often tell my students to ask themselves what it is that they are asking the reader to do. What energy are you expending, and what energy are you asking them to expend? Readers are already in an unfamiliar place in your poem. Don't make them open up a spreadsheet to keep track of where you are. Yes, Eliot wrote *The Waste Land* and you are welcome to write it too, but if you are not writing it, don't.

The new version of the poem became simpler in its mechanisms (location, mood, et cetera). Because it is simpler, it is also stranger. The dying brother has rented me this window. The elm runs its hand over the face of a brownstone. I walk among the furniture, thinking about living in Brooklyn, where all days feel like "dented Sundays."

I was writing from a lonely place, trying to free myself of certain negative relationships to the world and to people that had led me to the same bad places over and over. I did not yet know how, but things were changing. While the new poem had little to do with the museum, the *akari* that appeared several times in the original version, both too literal and too strained toward a false profundity, is one of the few elements that survived, along with the docent of night, an echo of one of those gracious, silent figures who patiently wait to guide us in museums, but only if we request their help.

                    At night my ideas

                                        sometimes glowed
                    a little and were manageable glowing units . . .

        By the light of one paper lantern I've drunk

                            seltzer with lemon in the dark.
                    I've asked docent of night
        of the sunken beneath the water cathedral

                        who knows
                    who knows where the sparrow falls?
                            Aloud I said sometimes a bomb

                        shows a certain
        precise concern.
                        Let's pass the night

                                    discussing for whom.

    There were many docents in the original version, all of them
laden with unearned significance. They have all now become one
docent, of night, that strange cathedral sunk beneath the water.

*

Many years later, I was asked to write a poem. Whenever this hap-
pens I still feel shocked, as if I have to be extremely careful in how
I respond in order not to remind whoever is doing the asking (and
paying) that this is an absurd idea. This poem was to be published
in a German newspaper, and I would be paid in euros. The only
stipulation was that I write about an artist to whom I felt a connec-

tion. I immediately knew I wanted to revisit Noguchi, and his museum, at least in my memory. I felt like there was still something there that I had never finished. As soon as I thought of writing this new poem, so much came flooding back to me: the gardens, the rocks, the sculptures, the drawings of playgrounds he had designed and which were never built.

So much of the material of that original, bad poem didn't make it, but in writing at that time, I had indelibly recorded for myself what I had noticed, experienced, felt, in those repeated visits. I didn't have to look to remember what I had written and seen. In a way, the writing of that original failed poem mainly helped me select, gather, and unconsciously treasure certain specific memories of the place. I don't have a particularly good visual memory, so for me, it was unexpected to be able to call up exact details from the museum.

Still, I was having a lot of trouble getting the actual poem started. I ordered *Listening to Stone,* a book about the life of Noguchi. It arrived with such daunting thickness I did not even open it. I knew Noguchi had been biracial, the son of a Japanese father (a poet) and an Irish mother. He had lived in both Japan and the United States, and died in 1988. Other than that, I knew basically nothing about his life. When the deadline for the German newspaper was nearly there, I put my hand on the book and silently prayed that some of its information would enter into me. I felt silly, but also hoped that it would help. This absurd and desperate moment became the beginning of the new poem.

I only opened the book once, with the vow to myself that wherever I placed my finger, I would use that phrase somewhere in the poem. Luckily, I settled on "rare blue mountain flowers."

*

Today, I got a package in the mail. It was the manuscript of my new book of poems, back from my editor, full of his tiny scrawl that I have come over the years to treasure. He didn't like this poem about Noguchi, which surprised me, not because I am surprised when someone doesn't like my poems (on the contrary), but because of the reason. I had thought this poem was quite clear, yet in his notes he wrote that he was confused, particularly about who the "you" was. "I'm a bit lost in the pronouns," he wrote, with characteristic tact:

> like a hero from a novel
>
> you have journeyed there by train
>
> to become contemporary
>
> as rare blue mountain flowers
>
> other bodies are with you too
>
> in a small dark room you are together watching
>
> the same movie about his life

Reading the poem again, I see the problem began several lines earlier. I keep saying "you," but it is not clear who I mean. It is clear to *me* that this "you" is a person visiting the museum, but I don't say that. It's not at all clear that I am talking about walking among the stones. Oh. After thinking about what I actually meant, I came up with a solution, to add a single word, "visitor."

> if you go there visitor you will see

in those stones the reflection

of whatever about your shadow nature

you need to discover with unstable

certainty flicker while outside

the wells in the garden . . .

I've read a lot of poems where a poet says *you* but means *I*. It's a poetic convention. It can even mean *he, she, it,* or *they*. A floating unspecified *you* can be a placeholder, TK (the mark used in journalistic writing to indicate that a fact will be looked up later). Which is okay. It might even hold a productively undefined space in the poem, a feeling of longing that is powerful precisely because it has not yet attached itself to a person in the world. The first poem I wrote that survived into my first book is called "Whoever You Are." I was obsessed with an unspecified *you*. There is a lack of precision there, as if I am holding a space, outlining something I have not begun to truly understand. The poems that worked delineated an absence and a desire with which we are all, I believe, familiar.

I often see this in my writing in process, pronouns floating untethered to any obvious referent. It is understandable, of course, to feel so confused while one is in process and figuring things out. But the poem can suffer from that lack of clarity of purpose.

Such a small fix, just adding *visitor*, as a direct address. And the subjunctive, which provides a concrete possibility, an invitation, as opposed to a presumption. I much prefer the idea that I am respectfully inviting someone rather than assuming.

This was, come to think of it, surely part of the problem with the original, very bad poem I wrote many years ago, which was more interested in projecting some version of myself onto the mind of a reader, who would hopefully feel a combination of pity and admiration. I did not come to them, to you, as the stranger I am.

Plus, I love the sound of the word *visitor*. I never really listened to it before. After all, the reader is a visitor to the poem. The problem, which my editor pointed out, made me ask: Who is the audience? Who is listening? Who is the poem for? All poems are questions. Or maybe they are negations (a pushing away, an opening up of a space) followed by questions. There is a Jewish mystical idea that God once filled all the space in the universe, and then, to know Himself, He withdrew and created a space, which is our reality. Our job is to find holiness within ourselves and reflect it back to Him. Maybe that too was a question: Can I be seen? Can you?

POEM FOR NOGUCHI

One morning I summoned the giant tome

it arrived by means so magical

I just put my open hand

down on it like a cloud

rests on the roof of a dark museum

full of stone teardrops

so smoothly carved they could not

have come from anywhere

but Obsidian Desert or an island

in the Emerald Sea he alone

by his dual nature could echolocate

if you go there visitor you will see

in those stones the reflection

of whatever about your shadow nature

you need to discover with unstable

certainty flicker while outside

the wells in the garden

forget dark attachments and remind

each other in the soft afternoon language

you are on an isthmus

like a hero from a novel

you have journeyed there by train

to become contemporary

as rare blue mountain flowers

other bodies are with you too

in a small dark room you are together watching

the same movie about his life

on a loop until the city

full of innovative playgrounds

he never built fills us

and again at last we are each

a child wandering this time happily alone

among the harmless shapes

that know whatever calm people know

(from *Father's Day*)

In spring 2004, I was on my way to a reading at a bookstore in Iowa City, the famed Prairie Lights. About halfway there, I pulled into a rest stop and saw I had missed a call from my parents. I climbed up on a picnic bench so I could catch a signal under the featureless sky, and facing a field of some crop that stretched out eternally, called them on my little black phone.

They sounded metallic and far. They said they had just gotten back from the doctor, and that my dad had a "small dot" in his brain, it was no big deal, it could be taken care of, I shouldn't worry. Sitting atop a picnic bench, holding the phone to my ear, I listened to them tell me everything would be fine. Only much later did I learn that they had just been told that my dad was assuredly going to die within the next year.

Many years before, when I told my dad I wanted to study to be a poet, we were driving. Cars are the best and worst places to deliver messages. One cannot not listen. He took the news in silence. The car rolled on, the landscape of the corridor between Baltimore and Washington, D.C., passing by in an unremarkable exurban blur. The figurative distance between us seemed to grow even more immense at that moment, and we sat without saying anything, without any real idea what the other was thinking, listening without listening.

*

I returned to New York, where it soon became clear that the situation was dire. Many hallucinatory months followed. I wandered around the city, and could no longer write. I often would go back to Maryland and live in my childhood bedroom for weeks, surrounded by photographs of myself in high school, rereading my favorite books from childhood, D'Aulaire's *Norse Gods and Giants*, Anne McCaffrey's *Dragondrums*, *Watership Down*. I hurt my back badly trying to pick my father up after he fell in the bath. He kept a catalog of wooden boats next to his bed, and often talked about building one. American elms tapped my window, just as they had in my childhood. I would go for long drives through Rock Creek Park, staring up at the great beech trees, hundreds of feet high.

My father died in the back room of our house in early 2006. I watched him take a final breath, more like a cough, then go to the underworld. I had nothing to say, not then, not at his funeral. As soon as I saw the simple wooden coffin, traditional in Jewish funerals, I put down my head and wept, wordlessly, for the entire service. Farewell. What is most important was never done, will never be completed.

A few weeks after his death I went back to New York and taught a workshop to some grumpy graduate students at the New School, who understandably were not that interested in my loss. All that miserable spring I automatically did whatever tasks were necessary during the day, then went out to get blindingly drunk, sleepwalking through my life. I couldn't talk about what I was feeling, because it seemed simultaneously too huge and utterly banal. Everyone either has a dead father, or will. I still could not write a word.

*

Meanwhile, my friend Joshua Beckman out in Seattle had a brilliant, lunatic idea: he convinced the publisher of Wave Books, where he was the editor and I worked remotely, part-time, to sponsor a trip through America and Canada for fifty days, giving readings, picking up and dropping off poets, reading with poets in the towns where we arrived, sleeping in the bus or on floors or wherever.

Thus the Poetry Bus, Joshua's quixotic vehicular dream. The idea was this: to somehow *do* something. Bring together people who would not otherwise be together through poetry. It was not very efficient, which was the point. It was an analog, biofueled attempt to connect the art we had devoted our life to making to the real conditions of the lives of others.

We left that September, looking bright and eager, and returned in late October as velocitized Bigfoots, only vaguely human. It would take many years to process what happened, all those encounters, seeing the art I love and dedicated my life to welcomed, misunderstood, disregarded, abused, treasured, ignored.

On the bus was a filmmaker I had at the last moment impulsively asked to come along. I had convinced a rightly wary Joshua this was a good idea. It turned out the filmmaker unfortunately fancied himself a Werner Herzog type, a skeptic and provocateur. It was vaguely hilarious but also disruptive and annoying to have someone around who thought it was his job to constantly ask if what we were doing was pointless, as if that had ever stopped occurring to us. He did have a gift for cinematography, and got some lovely shots of landscapes we were racing through. And he recorded many readings, documenting some wonderful, bizarre moments. He also had one very good idea that turned out to have a profound influence on me.

Somewhere along the way, he decided that each time we stopped to get gas or something to eat, he would go out and find a stranger and ask them if they wanted to hear a poem. If they said yes, which happened surprisingly often, he would go back on the bus, grab one of us, and film us standing next to that person, reading a poem, beside the roaring highway, all of us hearing the words disappear.

I found myself next to a much smaller man, a truck driver, at a rest stop somewhere. The wind was blowing hard, and the trucks and cars blasted along behind us. We both faced the camera, and I took out my book and tried to read to him, amid all the noise. I felt the absurd responsibility, at that moment, to make poetry matter. The attention of this stranger, whose shoulder I can still feel beside my own, was my responsibility. It was ludicrous and heightened and beautiful and awful and vital. I read the poem, barely audible above the sound of the highway, and shook the man's hand, and he climbed up a ladder back into his truck.

*

That night we stayed in a motel in Gallup, New Mexico, the El Rancho, built by the brother of the director D. W. Griffith. A lot of movie stars had stayed there when they were filming in the desert. Each room had some cinematic theme, giving it a seedy and sinister charm. Drunk poets were sprawled everywhere, under silvered photographs of forgotten stars. In the morning we heard that during the night one of the nonpoetry guests had died, someone elderly. We never saw the body leave the building, only the ambulance quietly pulling away.

Back on the bus the next day, I was thinking about what it would be like if the filmmaker asked me to read again. What would I say to whatever stranger chance selected, it could be anyone, in a way that would still be poetry, and completely direct and personal and respectful of their time and attention? I decided to start a poem as if I found myself there, at that imagined moment.

My father was gone, but no matter how I spoke, or to whom, I felt I was always speaking through to him, across the vastest divide. I was trying to cross over something, always knowing that by all logic and likelihood, there was no one still there, just molecules dispersed into other forms, or no form at all. This distance is like that between any poet and reader. I began to think of this focus of thought and feeling, which shimmered between a particular presence and complete absence, to be like a listening ghost.

Who am I speaking to? I came to realize, through writing the poem, it is the imagined listener. Someone sympathetically distant. Reader as ghost, poem as attempt to cross over vast impossible distance. I owe you respect and gratitude for whatever time. From then on, whenever I wrote, I imagined I was writing as if I were speaking to someone who was there, a however ghostly you.

AGLOW

Hello everyone, hello you. Here we are under this sky.
Where were you Tuesday? I was at the El Rancho Motel
in Gallup. Someone in one of the nameless rooms
was dying, slowly the ambulance came, just another step
towards the end. An older couple asked me
to capture them with a camera, gladly I rose and did
and then back to my chair. I thought of Paul Celan,
one of those poets everything happened to
strangely as it happens to everyone. In German
he wrote he rose three pain inches above the floor,

I don't understand but I understand. Did writing
in German make him a little part of whoever
set in motion the chain of people talking who pushed
his parents under the blue grasses of the Ukraine?
No. My name is Ukrainian and Ukrainians
watched as the Germans killed everyone
but six people with my name. Do you understand
me now? It hurts to be part of the chain and feel rusty
and also a tiny squeak now part of what makes
everything go. People talk a lot, the more they do
the less I remember in one of my rooms someone
is always dying. It doesn't spoil my time is what
spoils my time. No one can know what they've missed,
least of all my father who was building a beautiful boat
from a catalog and might still be. Sometimes I feel him
pushing a little bit on my lower back with a palm
made of ghost orchids and literal wind. Today
I'm holding onto holding onto what Neko Case called
that teenage feeling. She means one thing, I mean another,
I mean to say that just like when I was thirteen
it has been a hidden pleasure but mostly an awful pain
talking to you with a voice that pretends to be shy
and actually is, always in search of the question
that might make you ask me one in return.

(from *Come On All You Ghosts*)

The summer after we returned was when I met Sarah in Amherst. A
year later, I moved to San Francisco, where she lived and worked. I
had always loved New York, and every single morning when I still
lived there, I felt when I walked out the door that I had a small but
important part in some giant movie someone was making. Re-
turning to the Bay Area felt uncanny, like moving simultaneously
backward and forward in my life.

Right when I was moving, I got a job offer to teach for a semester in Houston. It seemed unwise to refuse. They were paying many times more than I had ever made, and it was a real job, or at least a stepping stone to one. In the heady spirit of a new relationship, Sarah and I decided we could not be apart for any long period of time, so I flew every week from San Francisco to Houston and back. This ensured gradual derangement, not to mention a draining of the bank account that made the whole exercise financially futile. After so much time in airports and rental cars, never being in any one place for longer than three or four days, the whole season became a shimmering hallucination. Whenever I was in one place I also felt I was in another, and I often found myself confused, walking through one doorway and ending up in a room in a different city.

Once, in the airport, I looked over and saw, walking next to me, Flavor Flav, with that overdetermined giant clock around his neck. I absently wondered if he had to take it off to go through security. Then I got on the plane and Santana was reading a paperback in first class, wearing his trademark bandanna. He gave me a big toothy smile, as if he agreed this whole simulation was hilarious.

That fall, two huge hurricanes came through Houston. The second shut down the entire city for several weeks. Driving through downtown I saw all the windows in the high-rises had been blown out, like someone had dropped a bomb. The city was deserted. For some reason the neighborhood where I was staying was the last in the entire city to get power restored. There was a heat wave, so I slept downstairs in the kitchen. Outside was a rotting swimming pool, a green malevolent eye.

A phrase started to come to me. Come on, all you ghosts. I thought it was a song lyric, or maybe something from someone else's poem, and I searched for it again and again, without results. On one of my last flights back from Houston I actually started to hear it in my head, as if a voice were saying it. There on the plane I knew that this was the title of the book I was working on, that this poem would be the last one in that book, that its form would be in tercets, and that it would be in five sections. I knew exactly how it would begin, and what would happen in each section.

I got off the plane and started writing the poem in my head in the car. Over the next few days I finished it, more like a transcribing:

I heard a little cough
in the room, and turned
but no one was there

except the flowers
Sarah bought me
and my death's head

glow in the dark key chain
that lights up and moans
when I press the button

on top of its skull
and the ghost
I shyly name Aglow.

Are you there Aglow
I said in my mind
reader, exactly the way

you just heard it
in yours about four
poem time units ago

unless you have already
put down the paper directly
after the mention

of poetry or ghosts.
Readers I am sorry
for some of you

this is not a novel.
Goodbye. Now it is just
us and the death's head

and the flowers and the ghost
in San Francisco thinking
together by means

of the ancient transmission device . . .

The phrase that bubbled up from my psyche was an incantation, a personal prayer. There was something about the rhythm of it that exactly embodied the form I needed for my thoughts, and what I was so intensely feeling. Its rhythm made a shape into which fit not only the poetry I needed to write, but how I needed to begin to live, now that my father was truly gone.

Poetry must have been invented early in human experience, around a fire or in a cave. As soon as we had language, we surely had the instinct to play with it, to see what else it could do besides just tell us the facts. "After great pain, a formal feeling comes," Emily Dickinson wrote. She is referring to that initial stage of grief, but for poets this can mean the compulsion to find the exact form in language that captures the pain, not through the meaning of the words, but through rhythm and sound and shape.

As I wrote my poem about my father, I felt my loss again become newly real. I moved through it, now with some distance, which paradoxically brought pain that was just as intense, but also a genuine perspective that I could not have had in the first years after my father's death. I thought also of the people I had passed in New York and Houston and San Francisco and in all those cities and towns we had driven through. Them, and also of my friends, many of whom were gone from my life or from life altogether. I knew I was talking to them, and hopefully perhaps, by extension, to you. Writing the poem reminded me that my continuing sorrow was not only not unique, but the most common thing in the world.

Here We Were Happy

It's very early and I'm upstairs, trying to be quiet so no one wakes up. I'm reading about the great redwoods that burned, and also about how they protect themselves. Their long, horizontally grooved, thick bark does not contain flammable resin. It protects the delicate sapwood inside. It's still dark, and I am thinking about these trees, how they survived another fire season, and how I don't have any desire to use them as any sort of metaphor.

Tomorrow I leave for some readings in Hawaii. I desperately hope to visit poet W. S. Merwin while I'm there. I've been invited by the organization dedicated to the preservation of his home on Maui, which he built with his own hands, and the forest of rare palms he planted that surrounds it. He still lives in there, in the house in the tiny village that actually really is named Haiku. I'm surrounded by toys, chaos, noise, obligations. He has lived for decades there, for a long time with his wife, Paula, now alone, putting stones down on the paths, clearing them off, planting species of palms that would otherwise be extinct, watching them grow over the years. Writing his poems there. He is past ninety, and cannot see any longer. He's one of the poets who changed everything for me when I first started writing. One time, in Seattle, I said hello and shook his hand, but I have never spoken to him. I'd like to sit with him for a little while, on the famous lanai I've heard others talk about, and just listen, before it is too late.

I can't seem to concentrate. There is too much to do, and I cannot seem to make contact with any energy of inspiration. The sky outside is getting lighter and soon it will be time to get him ready for school. I had put away this writing for a few moments to respond to some utterly urgent email from school that requires my immediate, full attention or else things will remain exactly as they are. Behind it as I was composing my thoughts into official form, I noticed a draft in my notes program that I cannot remember having written. Probably I began it at some stray moment on my phone.

we were not born to survive

we were born to live next to the hospital

all our good ideas

for fixing everything

permanently getting repaired

and what is it like to be that black and white dog

trotting happily alone past the doorway

I wonder which of the faces

does he belong to

or is someone in one of the windows looking down

from a little silver guillotine

This is obviously not yet a poem. Just notes. In the middle of "The River of Bees," from his 1967 book, *The Lice*, Merwin asks himself, "how shall I live." At the end of the poem, he reaches a door, upon which is written the line that I took as the first line of my draft:

We are the echo of the future

On the door it says what to do to survive
But we were not born to survive
Only to live

I can hear the irrefutable music in Merwin's lines. There is a deep wisdom there. "Only to live" is both accurate and ironic. *Only* to do the most difficult thing, to inhabit one's life, to truly live it. No such music is yet in my poem, and it does no good to steal his. Right now in my life I need to ask a different question, about a word so dangerous in its generality and abstraction: *love*. I try to work on the poem.

We were not born to survive.
Maybe we were born to love,
but what? That doesn't
sound right. Maybe
we were born to live
next to the translucent hospital.
Others pass through
and move further on
out of sight or return
with nothing to say except
soon it will be your turn.
Or we were born to live

under the first elm and carry
its shadow upon us
wherefore we go . . .

I can hear the mind creaking, like one of those early flying machines in which the maniacal inventor jumps off the cliff to his doom.

The draft wanders around to eventually settle, for some reason, on Rome. I have a memory of staying for a few weeks in Campo de' Fiori, near the center of the city. The most notable thing about Campo de' Fiori is its statue of Giordano Bruno (1548-1600), a cosmologist and freethinker who was burned at the stake in the very spot where his own statue now is.

Today I was born to carry
around the glint of this
miniature silver guillotine
which is the name for the mechanism
itself and also the way
the weighted and for some
reason I would like not
to think about angled blade
descends. And also for the way
a window looks down
on the square where they used
to hold executions not so
long ago. Now they sell
fruit and coffee from stalls
next to the statue of the astronomer
burned right in that place
at the stake for knowing
we were not born at the center,

and those stars are suns
with their own planets,
and who knows maybe even
their own astronomers.

Bruno was part of the Copernican change in consciousness, away from a (false) certainty that we are at the center of the universe. This change seems to have continued until today. I think we are still not ready to accept that truth. It is probably the source of our constant anxiety. What price have we paid, are we paying, to be correct about the universe? And who is this vague "we" who keeps appearing?

*

I first came across Merwin's poems in my first semester of my second year of graduate school in poetry. I had taken the advice of the great Polish poet and left Berkeley. Now I was back in Amherst, where I had gone to college. Everything was strangely familiar, the same places but with different people. Poetry had crept up on me while I was trying to be a scholar. Suddenly it had become unavoidable. And now I was here, trying, and mostly failing.

I would circulate among the small town's many bookstores in uneasy, restless boredom, standing before the same shelves of used poetry books that I and the many other poets in town had already scoured a million times, leaving only a few volumes of Kahlil Gibran and some old musty editions of obscure Victorian poets. One day I wandered into a hippie bookshop on Main Street called Beyond Words. Inside, it was dim and peaceful, and there were many candles collectively emitting the vague scent of promised enlightenment. Hidden speakers purred with low-volume zither. Most of the books were about spirituality, but upstairs was a small collection of poetry. Among them was an intriguing volume: *The Second Four Books of Poems*. This title seemed mystically specific and preordained, like a book a character would come across at the start of a quest. Naturally, I picked it up.

I was mostly unaware at the time of W. S. Merwin. On the back of that book, it said he had been born a long time ago (1927) and had won many prizes, including a Pulitzer. The jacket copy quoted Adrienne Rich's praises that in these poems "the silences . . . are as essential as the speech," and that the poems are "more open than ever," neither of which I understood. There was an aura about the whole package of the book—its black and gold colors, its weight, and the elegant yet unfussy serifs of its font—that compelled me. Maybe it was even a book of actual spells. I decided to break my usual rule and buy it new.

The first of the four books, *The Moving Target* (published in 1963), didn't leave me with an impression I remember, though it must have made me keep reading. It is no exaggeration to say that the second book, *The Lice*, was a life-changing revelation. The poems struck me with an immediate, present ghostiness. The poet was both completely there and also not. His poems were totally available and utterly strange. Yes, Adrienne, the silences were as essential as speech. They were more open than ever. How did he do this?

> Every year without knowing it I have passed the day
> When the last fires will wave to me
> And the silence will set out
> Tireless traveler
> Like the beam of a lightless star

What odd precision.

Virginia Woolf wrote that "the poet is always our contemporary," and in these thirty-year-old poems it was easy to feel a kind of timelessness that allowed a discrete speaker, me, to slip into them and feel I belonged in them, and they in turn belonged in my time. They still feel that way to me. Their abandonment of punctuation adds to these feelings. Not only does it create a paradoxically drifty precision, but it causes the poet to explore technical solutions of composition that give the poems an architectural solidity, without the sense that the poems are constantly being meddled with by their creator.

The poems in *The Lice* usually have identifiable situations, often described in the titles. While they can at times become thrillingly surrealistic ("The fist is coming out of the egg / The thermometers out of the mouths of the corpses"), they never abandon the reader, or lose their emotional way. Legendary, foundational proto–eco poems "The Last One" and "For a Coming Extinction" coexist with many powerful antiwar poems, including "The Asians Dying" and "When the War Is Over."

All poets look to their recent or distant predecessors to help us, to teach us what we need to know. At a crucial time, when I was lost and struggling as a poet, I came across Merwin, and saw the outlines of a way forward. In my own poems I was struggling to find a way between the possibilities of the material of language, its strange slippages and exciting collisions, and my desire to write poems that would not be esoteric, obscure. How to find a contemporary American idiom that would feel more noble than mere conversational speech, that could contain my various impulses and allow me to not only sound like my true self but also rise outside myself, and into other realms? The poems in *The Lice* were the ones I needed.

*

The Lice also showed me that great poetry could be reconciled with political engagement. Before I read Merwin, I thought the only way to be political was to be polemical, didactic, convinced, certain, which did not work for me. As soon as I talked about politics or really any social matter in my poetry, I became instantly strident. The poems became ugly and lifeless. Thankfully, I can't find any examples from my early work, but trust me, they were quite bad.

In his introduction to *The Second Four Books of Poems*, Merwin defends the right of poetry to be free of all obligation: "Poetry like speech itself is made out of paradox, contradiction, irresolvables. . . . It cannot be conscripted even into the service of good intentions." This idea sounded familiar to me. And yet, immediately after that passage, he explains the urgency he and his fellow poets feel to engage with the most troubling and pressing societal issues of their time:

> Poets have been known to be smug about their fine useless-
> ness, but the Vietnam War led many poets of my generation
> to try to use poetry to make something stop happening. We
> will never know whether all that we wrote shortened that
> nightmare by one hour, saved a single life or the leaves on
> one tree, but it seemed unthinkable to many of us not to
> make the attempt and not to use whatever talent we had in
> order to do it. In the process we produced a great many bad
> poems, but our opposition to that horror and degradation
> was more than an intellectual formulation, and sometimes it
> tapped depths of bewilderment, grief, rage, admiration, that
> took us by surprise. Occasionally it called forth writings that
> may be poems after all.

This was something new. And the poems in *The Lice* enacted that grief, rage, bewilderment, sorrow. They were poems of rage against war, against ecological destruction, against cruelty. I studied them to see how he could be simultaneously so ethical and open.

*

I somehow got to Hawaii, then fell into a dreamless sleep. I woke up on California time and sat down in the predawn darkness next to the water feature in the fancy hotel. Everyone who works here says hello, *mahalo*, a compensated *aloha*. Couldn't find a way to get from the infinity pool to the small silver (not sliver, it's still dark, predawn, just a little light from somewhere glittering off the silver sand) of beach, everything completely fenced off.

I go back to the hotel room, to reread *Summer Doorways*, Merwin's memoir of his early years. One of my favorite passages is one in which he writes about seeing houses that weren't there. He calls them "ghost houses." (A hotel is also a house that feels full of ghosts.) This idea of the ghost house is also central to the plot of *The Lost Domain* by Alain Fournier (in French, *Le grand Meaulnes*), a book I first read and barely understood in high school French class. There is a small pink edition from the Oxford Classics, in translation, which I love so much inside and out. In it, a young man runs away from a provincial boarding school and has a romantic adventure at a magical estate that he cannot locate again, until eventually he does.

Both times Merwin saw ghost houses, he was on outings with his father in the Pennsylvania countryside. When he left his father to explore, he came across them, and then when he brought his skeptical father back, they had disappeared. He describes seeing these houses with such detail, and such painful accuracy. You can feel how sure he was that they were there, and the implication in the text is that he might have been seeing what had been there long ago in the past, manifesting temporarily, just for him, in the present.

We went to see Merwin's palm garden, which is really a forest. They call it a garden because it's cultivated, but that makes it seem far less wild than it is. He planted every single palm, and placed all the stones on the paths. Now he is blind and mostly not mobile, often sleeping. He's written his final poems, after his wife died. She's buried under a black stone that says *Here We Were Happy*.

*

It seems so futile, this idea Merwin had decades ago, to bring all the nearly extinct species of palm trees here to this little place in Hawaii and preserve them. The comparison between that commitment and writing poetry made sense to him, and organized his life. That unity to his life still feels elusive to me, though I am sure it has to do not with planting trees, but with being a father.

I went for a walk with my editor, Michael, to an old shrine, the Ulupō Heiau. We stood under an immense tree. Michael talked about his family, how they are from a town called Ottawa, Illinois, now infamous. In the 1920s and 1930s, young women were employed by the Radium Dial Company to paint the faces of clocks and watches, to make them glow in the dark. To keep their brushes sharp enough to accurately paint on small surfaces, the women were instructed to suck on the tips. The factory owners knew from autopsies that these women were getting sick and dying, but denied it. All this, as well as how the women organized themselves into the "Society of the Living Dead" and fought back in court to establish safe working conditions, is described compellingly in a book by Kate Moore, *The Radium Girls: The Dark Story of America's Shining Women*.

Michael told me about his grandfather's sister, who was one of the first to die from radium poisoning from working at Radium Dial Company. We walked among the rubble of the shrine, and under the trees, and I listened.

Merwin was feeling good and wanted to see us. We went into the house, which in color and spirit seemed to be part of the surrounding forest, and sat on the lanai overlooking the palms. We talked about the property, about the buildings on it, about poets, like James Merrill, one of the sons of that famous fortune. Merwin went to Princeton, where he met Merrill in John Berryman's office. At one point Merwin forgot Merrill's name and called him "what's-his-name, the incredibly wealthy one." He talked about Galway Kinnell, who was at Princeton at the same time as Merwin (they both waited tables to make money while they were in school), about suicides and how when someone dies by suicide, their children often do as well. So, Merwin said, in a way, when you commit suicide you aren't just killing yourself.

At one point I saw a bird in a tree and I knew if I described it carefully enough he'd be able to tell us what it was. So I looked for a while, trying to remember everything, and then said, What is that bird with the gray feathers and orange beak and a little bit of red in its tail and a crown, and he said, That's a female cardinal, and I think she is about to have babies, so if we put a blueberry on the railing of the lanai, her mate, the red cardinal, will come and get it. Merwin put two blueberries on the railing and the red cardinal came.

All the time I was listening, I knew I could go back and finish the poem I had found before I left, the one that originally began with Merwin's line from *The Lice*. There is a certain feeling I have when I know how to finish a poem, that I finally have the experiences I need, that they will easily find their places in the poem.

Merwin was tired, and it was time to go. We took a few pictures, and I held his hand for a moment, then we walked out of the house, down the steps, and back into our cars. We stopped at a famous spot and watched some surfers. Everyone was impossibly fit. The waves were incredibly high and there were only a few brave or foolish surfers who had jumped off the black rocks covered in crosses mourning dead surfers and into the roiling water.

Then we had dinner at a place Obama apparently loves to go to, the Paia Fish Market. Michael told me you can order something known informally as an "Obama burger," just fish on a bun with wasabi. So Obama. Then I came back to the hotel, finished the poem, and had another dinner of fish. I'll become one soon, and swim away.

*

The problem with the poem for Merwin had been that I was not yet listening. I had not yet arrived where I needed to be. My own voice was too strong in my head. Once I listened to Merwin, and the silence of the palm garden that is not really silent at all, I was able to move the poem out of myself, and into some far more necessary space.

The poem got longer and more drifty and also more specific, more personal and less so, more in the moment (about something I had just done, an event) and also detached from this particular moment I was experiencing.

Today I read Merwin, his poems and his memoir. I thought about Merwin's poems and talked about them with people. I went to Merwin's house, sat on his lanai, said a few words, listened to him, described a bird to him, watched him feed a bird blueberries, heard him talk about Berryman and Kinnell and Merrill. Finished a poem about Merwin that, while it sounds like me, certainly also sounds a bit like Merwin, which I think is okay, I am so grateful to him, it is more than fine with me if my voice is just an overt near echo of his for a little while.

What kind of day was today? An anniversary. A tribute. A hiatus. A calming. A worry. A peace. I jumped in the pool many times, so many times it wasn't even cold anymore. Here we were happy. To live well would be to be able to write on a gravestone, a long time from now, *Here We Were Happy*, or, as Gerald Stern wrote in his great poem, *Lucky Life*.

POEM FOR MERWIN, AFTER VISITING THE PALM GARDEN

for a long time you planted one every day
and now the garden is a clock on forest time

forest time where we were happy
for a few translucent hours moving
into the ghost houses
no longer there

and the shade houses
that are
their myth of air

and the places where people used to gather
by the stream that is now a dry bed
to eat and sing
we cannot almost hear them

then out along the narrow paths
over stones I kept forgetting
like years you had placed

and the dead clock face painters
covered in radium could not convey
their messages to us
here in the permanent shade

the palms with their very different leaves
and seed pods seem to say

you who think nothing can be repaired

you who will not ever
be able to describe our shapes
and say I love to no one

or today I was born

you burned astronomers
look at our wet leaves
maybe you were not even born
for knowing your own planets

you were not born for knowing
but saying

a piece of wood burned next to the little jade statue
means no matter how many times we leave
we will keep returning

it means no matter how many times we go
out where they sell executions

we will come back here
where the black gravestone
is a window in love with the beloved

on it is written here we were happy
which is true

reading it I would like to remember
what I am feeling now
that I would like not to be
the mechanism

a blade angled in reason

I too would like to lay down
in my own sort of field
green with potential love

today I know I was born
to try to remember
the name of the simplest leaf

from the tree of my childhood

I have always known that god all along

and that we were each born
the shadow of reality upon us

so be not easily angry
pick up the small rose book
with its disappearing house on the cover

enter its doorway
get lost for a while

forget we were born to carry our names

until it is our turn with nothing to say
except we were born to love

and move further on

(from *Father's Day*)

Final Draft (Two Sleeps)

We walked out of Merwin's palm forest, and the caretakers placed a few small, round red seeds into our open hands. The seeds were a little heavier than I expected. I put them in my pocket and hoped no airport security agent would ask me what they were.

We had learned the names of all the palm trees, where they had come from. Many would be extinct if they were not here, on an island, in this valley where palms do not usually grow. For thirty years Merwin had been planting seeds brought here from all over the world, making a home for them. Did he dream of this place, and of it turning out this way? Did it begin with an impulse to save one tree, and then become an entire forest? Soon he would be gone, and this unlikely place, so strange, would be in all of our care.

I was there with Lew Hyde. Lew wrote *The Gift*, a book that artists know about and pass around. If you say you haven't read it, someone will soon hand it to you. It's about how art-making has always been a different economy, one that transcends and subtly challenges ordinary, destructive ideas of value. We entered dark auditoriums and sat next to each other in plush chairs. I read and talked a bit about poetry, staring into the darkness, then looking down at my book, wondering if I was saying anything useful. When Lew spoke, his words seemed to emerge in entire paragraphs that hung with golden lucidity in the air.

Today Lew wrote me an email: "Palm tree seeds lie on my desk. I'll probably take them to Costa Rica to see if my step-son can grow them in that hot climate." I tried to remember where I had put my own. They said, placing two red seeds in my hand, that I should keep them somewhere with very little light. Where did I decide that was? I think (I hope) in the closet in the kitchen, filled with things we rarely use but someday might.

I wrote him right back, "My palm seeds are in a dark closet, but we are making space for them in the new garden." Something about those words reminded me of that poem I began, so many months ago, using as seeds the words I had said to my son. I started with that phrase, two sleeps, and wrote outward from it, backward and forward, into the past and the future at the same time.

It's time to take the poem out of the drawer, the one I had managed mostly to forget. I am ready to take it apart again, and secretly, to go to work on it. The room is calm now. Simon is at school, Sarah is at work. It's a gray day, and the light inside the room is indistinguishable from the gray sky behind the trees, once again silhouettes. The day is soft and neutral and full of potential. "Like seeds in a dark closet / waiting for the new garden."

TWO SLEEPS

like seeds in a dark closet
waiting for the new garden
your poems with white light
your shadow poems
fill me with the same yellow glow
~~with~~ that tired old despair song
it hurts to read
your mostly forgotten poems
grand and disused
full of terrible cries
the dead make
buried under a tree
near ~~Alfacar~~
they rise upward
toward the constant death
of clouds whose names
we cannot know

When a comparison begins a poem, it creates some momentum. An isolated statement can feel inert—"Seeds in a dark closet / wait for the new garden" is an observation, to be received. The "like" that begins this poem opens up the mechanism, revealing the imaginative work of the poet, hopefully drawing the reader into the poem's movement. Ideally, a desire is created in the reader to move down the page and discover the completion of the comparison.

The "you" in this draft is Vicente Aleixandre, the Spanish poet and friend of Lorca whom Lew translated in a red book that collects his work. Before I left I had been reading it in preparation for our conversations, though these poems never came up. Aleixandre's simple, mysterious, confident, clear titles—"Song to a Dead Girl," "I Am Destiny," "We Feed on Shadow," "Close to Death," "Who I Write For," "The Tree"—fill me with dreamy envy.

Aleixandre won the Nobel Prize in 1977. Unlike Lorca, he lived through the horrors of the Spanish Civil War, then watched his country disintegrate into the sort of fascism that seems as if it would please many of our current leaders.

In his Nobel acceptance speech, he writes that some poets are focused on narrower concerns. They devote themselves "to exquisite and limited subjects." Others "turn to what is enduring in man . . . to that which essentially unites." He doesn't say one is better than the other, but that he himself belongs to the latter, is drawn to those larger subjects, to what connects us.

I feel, shyly, that I too count myself among those who want to speak to the primary, what is elemental, what unites. An old-fashioned hope, probably the final exhalations of an outdated humanism. Nevertheless, I'd like to find what is common between me, you, everyone, without eliding the essential distinctions.

In "Who I Write For," Aleixandre says his poems are for everyone: for the man who collapsed when he finally asked his question, for the people who don't read, for the dead woman and the dead children, for the murderer. For the reader who reads these words without desire. I have addressed my poem to him, for now, though I suspect that is only a bridge to something else.

*

In some old issue of the *New Yorker* I came across an article about artificial intelligence and, for an instant, finally understand how it all works. The collectors of information and monetizers of our attention are not collecting our bits of data from social media and our emails and searches and everywhere else, merely so they can sell us what we think we want. After all, how many different things do people actually want? They don't need to overhear our conversations to know we want shoes, phones, baby gates, the latest masks.

The aggregation of all this data about what we search for, buy, decide, report, etc., can, in immense quantities become, essentially, predictive. Something very close to objective truth. A dangerous *we*.

These are the mirrors held up to the future, in which are reflected vast forces that we cannot see. We are holding them up for those who can look at them and decide our fates. I see this, an actual vision, and it frightens me. Oh, how convenient to know everything when we want to know it. But how soon, if not already, whatever someone needs to figure out or predict can be discovered or foretold. Soon that *we*, or at least our machines, will know everything. They might even discover and reveal our own true desires, which will surely be terrifying.

Sitting at my desk, looking at the gray sky, I once again feel that aforementioned childish hope, that at the very least all this intelligence could help us predict where fires are going to start, so we can put them out before they rage for days and days. That would be a lot, and even so, surely not worth what we are giving up, as if we could choose.

TWO SLEEPS   ARTIFICIAL INTELLIGENCE

like seeds in a dark closet
waitng for the new garden

your poems filled
with light

fill me too
two sleeps

in the room behind me
and my fear

my son won't go
up the hill

with the others
somewhat awake

I sit writing you, stranger
within the same warm yellow glow

dispassionate conductors
guide their lonely passengers by

it almost hurts too much
to read your forgotten poems

grand and disused
as a terminal

full of terrible cries
the dead and living make

and it definitely hurts
to read how true

that already we are gathering
all the decisions

and the sound of machines
south of here

in the desert we cannot name
metal trees

rise upward toward the constant death
of clouds whose names

we all too soon will know

                    for V.A.

This most recent draft is getting somewhere, but is not yet right. I see I've put it in couplets, just to slow it down. So many of the poems I have written over the past few years are in a quick, columnar form, often without punctuation. I am drawn, physically, to writing that way. It *feels* right. But I wonder what I would say if I pushed myself into a different design.

Something about this poem seems to require a much different pace. I might also have unfortunately been trying to make it seem a bit more "poetic," by putting it in stately couplets, thereby giving it some authenticating white space to compensate for the fact that it was still anecdotal and a bit slow. But this only revealed that there was something missing.

I needed to let go of most of what was in the earlier drafts: the metaphors, the description of the men using machines to build that building across the street (so much taller now than it was when I first wrote those words), the clouds that I suspected were just a placeholder. So many things that seemed vital in the early stages of writing are gone. Only some ghostly adherence remains.

So many things happen to a person, are thought and said, and only some of them glow. Something glows off the page or out of life, and it is taken into the poem. Each poet will find things the others cannot. The challenge for each poet, each time, is finding the structure of poems that can further activate and extend these private intuitions of significance, into some kind of a tentatively collective realm. The poems are where the transition from private emotion into public myth, from the idiosyncratic into the collective symbol, and vice versa, is made. This is what Aleixandre calls the "pure nakedness radiating immutably from beneath [our] tired vestments." Where "the voice of the collective" is, in the individual voice, heard, and where, when we hear "we," each of us can find ourselves.

Like the word *we*, the lyric poem can so easily, under the banner of universality, become exclusionary. But I also believe, because

I have seen it, that poems can touch the universal in us not only without erasing our differences, but by celebrating those differences, and also finding our commonalities in language.

As appealing as it sounds, perhaps Aleixandre's distinction between poets of particularity and poets of commonality is false. All poets have something of both in them. "All poets are Jews," said Marina Tsvetaeva, shimmering irresolvably between metonymy and metaphor. All poets are as Jews are to everyone else, wandering the earth, looking for a home, linked only by the book and the primal myths written in it. They are by nature exiles from the society in which they live, connected far more to each other than to their fellow citizens, by language and books, an allegiance deeper and more lasting than mere nationality.

Poets are strangers to the dominant culture, uneasy guests. As much as we might love words, we are also deeply skeptical of them, and need to constantly examine and worry away at the very way of speaking that others take for granted. This binds poets to each other, across all divides. To grow as a poet, one must discover one's position in relation to the dominant language. I never know what it was like for each of my students to grow up, learn language, come to see themselves in relation to the authorities. What it is like for them now. I hardly know what it is like for myself.

ARTIFICIAL INTELLIGENCE

Like seeds in a dark closet
waiting for the new garden,
your poems filled me
with light filled me too.
Somewhat awake
I sit throwing these words
into your grave.
Once famous stranger,
it almost hurts too much
to read your forgotten poems,
grand and disuded
as a terminal.
The dead and the living
make terrible cries.
And it definitely hurts
to listen to the earth
say nothing.
This year was serious
in a dumb way, and vice versa,
dreams constantly
died without names.
One whose name
will become dust
said only two children died,
so it was a good year.
What can we say?
The word custody
gravely sparkles
and now we know
what no one born
was meant to know.

I hear him singing downstairs. This time, it's a song called "Many Pretty Trees All Around the World," by Ella Jenkins. Jenkins was born in 1924, and is still alive, at least as of this writing. She started writing songs for children in the 1950s. She adapted the call-and-response form of songs from the blues, from the Black churches in Chicago's South Side, and from many native cultures. Her songs invite participation and listening. Her voice is strong and clear, like my son's.

The song starts with humming of the melody, so that everyone can hear it, then whistling, so we can all hear it again. There are many pretty trees all around the world, here's a pretty tree now. It's an oak tree. It's an elm tree. It's a birch, a pine, a palm, a eucalyptus, a cedar. She sings, and we repeat the name of each tree, naming and holding it in our minds. In the recording, the song fades out, which makes it feel like it will go on forever.

His singing resonates through the house. Have I said enough how much I adore, and admire, his voice? His perfect pitch? His drawings? His persistence? His cheerful willingness to try, again and again? His spirit of enthusiasm, even when he is tired or overwhelmed? His joyful attachment to the people he trusts?

Together, he and I are building a world that is only partially composed of language. There is also song, building, drawing, long periods of comfortable silence. When I used to pick him up from school, I would ask him questions, and he would ignore me. Then he began to say, "I don't want to talk yet." Now he says, "Can I just enjoy the ride?"

*

I am always in danger of sleepwalking, of asking the wrong questions. Like, what can we do to help him fit in more to the world? Yes, it's dangerous for him not to fit in. Yes, of course, I don't want him to be lonely, I want him to have satisfying work, I want him to be intellectually and emotionally engaged, to love and be loved . . . I want I want I want. Of course I want. He is my son. I want everything for him, and now that he is here in the world there is nothing in the world I want that is not for him.

Here is a better question: What world can we make where he can thrive? That's not just a question for people who are not typical. It is the most important existential question for our species. What world can we imagine, and then make, where we *all* can live? Perhaps I sound like an anachronistic surrealist, but I really do believe, as deeply as I believe anything, that until we can recover our imaginations, we will continue to commit unimaginably cruel acts upon each other, and destroy everything around us.

What is beautiful to us—what we love—comes to us, unbidden. A line of poetry, or a child, or a question. We cannot know the tree from which it came. Our job is to build a new tree, a poem, or a world, in which it can thrive. Maybe that is what poets can teach the species. A treasure of a line, or image, or symbol, or word, needs a poem so that it can be truly seen and perceived, so it can thrive. Just like each of us and everyone.

At last we must start with what is beautiful and true—people, and animals, and nature, and the beautiful things humans have made—and begin to imagine what sort of structure would allow those things to be preserved and to thrive. We exist in an inescapable network of mutuality. How easy this is to forget. Anyone who lives on earth must never be considered an outsider anywhere. Anyone who lives in the world belongs to the world.

*

When you fall into the imagination of another person, in the reading of a poem, you are admitted to an intimacy. And you give your intimacy to that person too, whether or not you know it. The poem is a recognition of the difference and separateness of someone else's imagination, along with a simultaneous demonstration of the possibility of communion.

To experience this paradox is the gift and sometimes difficult pleasure of reading a poem, and writing it. The love you feel for a person or poem increases your tolerance, acceptance, and ability to see all people. Acceptance of difference no longer becomes a superficial matter of ideology, but a fundamental quality of being human, like breathing, from which it would be impossible to escape if you even wanted to. What is the worst thing that could happen? That you would feel compassion for a terrible person? For yourself? That you might see that even in the worst of us there is something at least to pity, and that this pity does not weaken us? It does not weaken us. On the contrary.

What we hear in poems is something we already know. As is so often the case, another poet says it best, in this case Mary Ruefle: "I used to think I wrote because there was something I wanted to say. Then I thought, 'I will continue to write because I have not yet said what I wanted to say'; but I know now I continue to write because I have not yet heard what I have been listening to."

I have not yet truly heard what I have been listening to. It is always there, most often hidden from me. I write to hear it. I write so I can keep dreaming a little while I am awake.

*

The seeds I was given did not belong in this poem, though the word *closet* does. I have heard that somewhere in the arctic there is a so-called bank, where they keep all the seeds in case of apocalypse. There seem to be many immediate flaws in this plan, including but not limited to planning for and therefore acknowledging an unacceptable eventuality, but doing it is probably better than not.

I like the word *closet* better than *bank*, it feels more accurate. I realize that lending and keeping safe are things that banks do, but they do a lot of other things as well that have nothing to do with what this repository of seeds is for. It is not merely that the analogy is partial. In fact, many of the things that banks do are at least indirectly responsible for the very situation that, god forbid, could require the use of these unremarkable seeds, laden now with significance and responsibility. I prefer a closet, where clothes or other objects wait patiently in the dark, out of sight until they are needed.

I watched a video of one of the president's minions, or maybe it was the president himself, saying that "only" two children in the camps at our southern borders had, in our custody, died this year. And that this was not bad, maybe even well done, maybe even deserving of a little praise. I recall it being said under an umbrella, in the rain.

The question that is too obvious to ask, that should eternally shame anyone who had to ask, is how many dead children would be too many? There is only one answer to that question. Once you start counting you are already doomed.

When the person under the umbrella made his remarks, the word *custody* stood out to me. I looked it up. *Custody* comes from Latin, and means both a state of being in the care of someone, and also being confined by them. That one word can mean both things testifies to the shifting border between those states, and the dangerous, parental ambiguity. Which form of custody will we choose?

After so many months, after I had given up, the poem that began as "Two Sleeps," which slept in a drawer and then was taken out, is done. I title it "Our Custody." The tentative, vital "we" in the poem really is all of us, whether we watch with helpless horror or indifference or tolerance or terrible glee.

For so long the drafts were about my son, like many others I have written since he was born. But every time I tried in "Two Sleeps" to write about him and my worries, I felt dissatisfied and solipsistic. I felt a lack of courage in myself, but could not identify my terror. I wrote even more about him and my fears. I thought it might be something I was trying to avoid. No. The poem was not about him, or Vicente Aleixandre, or artificial intelligence, or buildings or clouds.

At last I realized the source of the sick feeling I had all along. I had been too afraid to visualize those children in those detention centers, alone, without their parents, how confused and frightened they must feel. I think especially of the autistic children who must surely be there. They must feel so terribly lonely and afraid. It is almost beyond imagining, but we must. Like so many of us, I am afraid for them, and for my own helplessness, ashamed that no one can seem to find a way to stop this. In this case, there really is a collective responsibility, one that goes beyond sorrow, anger, outrage, blame, and grief. We might try to deny it, but we have all abandoned them, and in the poem, I want to live in that failure, without any comforting delusions. There is no place to hide, not in anger or conviction or in one's former certainty.

Our Custody

This year was serious
in a dumb way,
and hilarious
like a grave cut
into a smile.
Dreams constantly
died without names.
We listened to the earth
say nothing, and knew
everything.
The earth a grave
we throw words into.
Seeds in a dark
arctic closet
wait for the new garden
tended by machines.
One whose name
will become dust said
in the shadow
under an umbrella
in our custody
only two died,
so it was a good year.
What can we say?
They were children
and will always be.

I tried so many times to write the beginning of this book, in order to explain what I was doing: why I was writing this one poem, sharing its drafts, telling the story of how I got here. It never felt right. The tone was either too obscure, or impersonal, or melodramatic, or self-absorbed. Until I listened, and, letting go of the "I," wrote it down as if it were being told to me. That is why this book begins in the third person. "I is another," Rimbaud wrote in a letter, and to try to tell my own story and listen to it as if I were another was the only way it felt true to me.

When I began this book, it was a season of terrible fires. I started to write a new poem, "Two Sleeps," and to show my work as I made it. I wrote every day for many months. I worked on the poem, then put it away, then came back to it again. I wrote about my life at the time, my fears, my memories. Other new poems came. I talked about poems from the past. In the midst of all this anger and conflict, I so often felt foolish working on the poem, and writing about writing it, while also knowing that was what I had to do.

The poem I started writing at the beginning of the book went through many drafts, and ended up somewhere unrecognizable from its origins. It all seemed part of a larger story. Somehow, I finished the poem, though almost everything about it changed. I felt as if I had completed something important, and also that old questions remained, and new ones were already arising.

Writing in sobriety, in desperation, I felt a constant desire to reach out, to connect with others, to break through isolation. To be a poet of the particular, and also of commonality, of that which unites. I hope you will hear echoes of your story in mine. Probably, I am just going to keep telling this story, again and again, trying to fully understand, which I never will.

*

Paul Valéry wrote that a poem is never finished, only abandoned, which is just as true for a book. And yet, there is something about the final, complete version. A click. Not as if great problems have been solved, which is of course impossible, but as if they are, at least for a moment, visible.

Each time I finish a poem, a book, I want to begin again. I heard that click of finality, which as much as an ending equally resembles the sound of a new door being opened. Terrance Hayes: "the best way to combat / Sadness was to make your sadness a door." I agree with Alejandra Pizarnik: "It is not true that poetry resolves enigmas. Nothing resolves enigmas." But she goes on to say, and this gives me great hope, that "to formulate them by way of the poem . . . is to unveil them, to disclose them. Only in this way can poetic inquiry become an answer: if we are willing to risk that the answer become a question."

Or as James Baldwin put it: "The artist cannot and must not take anything for granted, but must drive to the heart of every answer and expose the question the answer hides."

While I was writing this book, something strange, and also perhaps utterly predictable, happened. I was writing a book of prose to contain one poem, and also to show the process of making it. But in writing this prose, certain phrases, images, scraps of language remembered or imagined or heard began to take on a familiar, undeniable glow. These stayed in my mind, often visiting me in my sleep. They formed the scaffold of a new poem, one filled with the experiences, memories, images, ideas remembered and revealed, intertwined with concerns beyond my own personal struggles and dilemmas. And that is how I'll end this book.

I fear that ending with a poem of environmental fear, of masks and runaway technology, of helplessness in the face of power and the helplessness even of power in the face of forces at last unleashed, I will primarily reflect a feeling of hopelessness and doom. If so, that is only part of how I feel. I also feel hope.

Audre Lorde wrote that poetry "lays the foundations for a future of change, a bridge across our fears of what has never been before." I would like to straggle across that bridge with you, over our fears, so we can be alone together, near each other, moving toward something new.

FINAL PRIVACY SONG

I woke up in California
wondering, can
all this information
they are teaching
to teach itself put out
these autumn fires
before they begin.
I can see figures
walk up the hill,
not wearing their masks.
Here in this room
let the smoke
for an hour
be forgotten,
I don't want to listen
to my breathing anymore.
And when I die
please bury me
underneath an old oak
near the train
in sleep city
and do not tell
the ones who see me
through this screen
where I've gone.

All morning I sat
breathing filtered air.
Above me they
were sleeping,
then they were not.
There was wailing
then much frenzied joy.
The great magnolia
through the umber
watched him
go to school
in his mask,
wearing his shoes
that light up when
you step down hard.
Already she travels
across the new bridge
to meet a demon
who built
a lucrative portal.
He wants now
to construct a hall
named for his father,
a master of oil,
and fill it forever
with old music.
Each time
someone reaches
through the void
another imagined
coin is born,
even after you die
the cypher lives on,
a few electrons
to some blade
in a server
forever cling.

The lonesome
endless whistle
travels north
along the bay,
that sound
journeys
many miles
to all our ears
no matter how high
in a valley
or deep
in a cloud
of our own making
we pretend
separated to live.
I hear it now.
All these years
I never noticed
until he said
do you hear
that sound,
we stopped
and listened then
returned to building
our towers
to the skies.
Under Mission,
under the Armory
under the silent buses
with tinted windows
there is a river
they call a creek
that really does still flow,
you can read about it
in a book called
Vanished Waters.
Over it knowledge

workers ride
south to sit
behind giant blue
panes that hang
in the buildings.
Calm new questions
are asked.
How many metal trees
to reverse the past
should we plant
in the desert
where only spirits go?
Can they learn
to breathe smoke?
I got a ride here
one September
just in time
to miss the end
of the quiet age.
We drew the names
of our bands
with black sharpies
we stole from the office
of someone's dad,
then hung posters
in constant
anachronistic rain.
No matter how much
din we made
no one could hear.
Under the perfectly
damaged hues
of our hair we knew
we would meet
at the crumbling palace,
the walls flickered
unwatchable films

of films by friends
of friends inhabiting
dingily grand
apartments the landlords
barely remembered
they owned,
dusty chandeliers
swayed above
meticulous cabinetry
in every harmless quake,
those rooms, who
lives in them now?
In one I slept
surrounded
by walls someone
before me had painted
a particular orange
even fire dreads,
the color just after
the sun beneath
the horizon has
permanently disappeared.
I closed my eyes
to cross the famous
bridge, moving
north toward
the redwoods.
And no one said
far too late
don't fall asleep
in the dream.
Each morning past
the now dark bars
our manic joy so
lit up just a few hours
ago we'd move
toward our jobs

inside a purely personal
cloud without
knowing we walked
through ghost villages
on the banks
of the creek
a thousand years
before the settlers
came and gave the lake
a new name, Dolores.
Now it's a sad
waterless pool
full of human toys,
scientifically lonely
with forever
unrequited desire
for us to remember
the Ohlone lived here
until they were taken
north in little boats
across the bay
to build their own hospital
where they could die
from our disease.
One day my dad
on business
flew in for an hour,
he took me
to an establishment
that glittered
every surface
with available joy,
then remarked
you have no door.
Then we went up
the famous wooden stairs
to that room where

you can still talk
to the dead,
hear that old song
its dark secret answer
and look down
on the city
with those windows
that seem to know
no moment
can ever remain.
For a pitiless moment
I saw him
just as he once
stood in that very place
with my uncle
when he was young.
We embraced
in the requisite
gold sunset
then he went back
across the country
to where I never
grew up under
Maryland elms.
Now he is wherever
those spirits who sat
with us during
those extinct afternoons
of doing nothing
have gone, leaving
us under these
black clouds.
When I die
please turn me
into an old oak,
spreading my branches
holding the cameras

and do not tell them
where I've gone.
I read the news,
it does not deliver
what I need
every moment
not to die,
so I pick up
the blue book
that knows
a thousand years ago
a poet slept face down
on a table
just like this one
until Feng Seven found him,
then he said
(Feng wrote it down)
the sleeves of poetry
are wet with amber
tears and false wine,
smeared calligraphy
spelling out these
immortal words:
I am the drunken echo
of lovers in the tower,
deliver me
to the Emperor
or throw me in the fire,
or best of all
tie me to an arrow
and shoot me
into the yard
of that beautiful widow
who moved away
so long ago only
the tall abandoned weeds
remember, shoot me

into the yard
so I can talk about her
to the tall
abandoned weeds.
He said I know
these immortality pills
are killing me
but I take them anyway,
there's no time
left to learn the sword,
can you hear
the truant wind
so green
say the door
to the great rebellion
is almost here
so let's drink our despair
until that final
morning of sick rain
before the civil war.
He said it into the same
silence of the candle
that comes to me now,
a storm carried
through the window,
eerie music of the hour,
is it coming from the leaves?
The rain is almost here.
Cellos leak
to that same darkness,
to that same darkness
a golden door.
At last the smoke
is blowing out through
the gate to the sea.
I hear the Emperor
shift in his bed.

He can't remember
who he ordered
to watch us
or the name
in which we did
all these things
written on this glowing
light emitting
diode doom scroll
I am looking down on
here at the end
as it moves
endlessly down.
O analytical daylight
I hear the old song
that says we were born
when we fell asleep
next to each other
under those huge
nameless trees
that when they burn
will not return no matter
what we invent or
how alive and strong
they look to us in dusk.

Acknowledgments

I would like to thank the following people, who were patient and kind, who read various versions of the manuscript or just fielded my panicked calls and texts, and who most of all have been steadfast and unwavering in support of me and our family:

Catherine Barnett, Matt Rohrer, Ada Limón, Travis Nichols, Brenda Hillman, Robert Hass, Leni Zumas, Robert Casper, Mary Beth Meehan, Joshua Beckman, Chicu Reddy, Alexandra Zapruder, Michael Zapruder, Marjorie Zapruder, Deborah Landau, Charles Bissell, Tim Maxwell, David Shields, Amy Gerstler, Marilyn Abildskov, Gabriel Kahane, Paul Lacinski, Ralph Savarese, Naomi Kanakia. Special thanks to Bill Clegg, with whom I hatched this idea in the first place.

Thank you, Major, Ada, and Camille, for your constant friendship and laughter in these days, zero and otherwise.

In particular I would like to thank, with love and admiration, Steve Almond and Emily Rapp Black, who each with inexhaustible patience read several drafts of this book and provided crucial editorial guidance, along with their warmth and friendship and support.

My great gratitude to Oscar Villalon, Nadja Spiegelman, and Christopher Beha, who edited sections of this book that appeared in *Zyzzyva*, *Paris Review*, and *Harper's*. "Final Privacy Song" was first published in *Zyzzyva*. Immense gratitude as well to my editor at Copper Canyon, Michael Wiegers, who has always been a reader, supporter, interlocutor, and friend to me and my poems.

Thank you to Olivia Taylor Smith, Chris Heiser, and Allison Miriam Smith at Unnamed Press, for your faith in this book, your essential editing, and your support and friendship. So much thanks to Jaya Nicely for her amazing design, and to Laura Cherkas, for rescuing me at the end with final editing, catching so many errors and repetitions and infelicities. Any that remain are my fault alone.

Special gratitude to composer Gabriel Kahane, who asked me to write the text for a musical composition that eventually became "Final Privacy Song." His collaboration, editing, and exhortations for clarity and weirdness and singable lines were all essential to the writing of this poem.

Thank you and farewell to James Tate, Tomaž Šalamun, and Dean Young.

Most of all, thank you to Sarah and Simon. I love you both, and our family.

Permissions